Mediterranean Diet for Women Over 50

One Year of Quick, Famous and Easy Mouth- Watering Recipes that Busy and Novice Can Cook. Lose up to 15 Pounds in 3 Weeks.

AUTHOR
CLAIRE MILLER

Table of Contents

What Is The Mediterranean Diet?

The Mediterranean diet is based on traditional products that they ate mainly in the 60s around the Mediterranean in some nations such as Italy and Greece.

That piece of information about the 60s is crucial since they nowadays eat a lot of pasta and pizzas, which in turn is not really good for health.

Researchers see that these people were particularly healthy compared to most Westerners and had a low risk of most lifestyle diseases. Various studies showed that the Mediterranean diet could cause weight loss and avert heart attacks, strokes, type 2 diabetes, and premature death.

Please note: there is no right way to follow the Mediterranean diet, as there are many Mediterranean countries, and people in different areas may have eaten different types of food. So there is not merely one type of Mediterranean diet.

How is the diet structured?

To know what makes the diet so healthy, it is first wise to understand how the menu is structured and which products you should mainly eat and which you should avoid.

Which foods exactly belong to the Mediterranean diet is a bit controversial, partly because there is so much variation between the different countries. Yet, there are plenty of the same products that form the basis of the Mediterranean diet in different countries.

Which products should form the basis of your diet?

The premise of the diet is developed by unprocessed products. These products can, therefore, be found in nature.

The diet used in most studies is rich in healthy plant-based foods and contains relatively few animal products. However, eating a menu like fish and seafood is advised at least twice a week.

The Mediterranean lifestyle also means that you exercise regularly, that you share meals with other people and that you enjoy life.

The basic products include:

• Vegetables: broccoli, cabbages, onions, cauliflower, carrots, sprouts, spinach cucumber, and tomatoes

• Fruit: avocados, apples, oranges, pears, strawberries, grapes, bananas, melons, peaches, dates, and figs

• Nuts: walnuts, almonds, cashews, macadamia nuts

• Seeds: sunflower seed, pumpkin seed, and linseed

• Legumes: all kinds of beans, lentils, chickpeas, peanuts

- Potatoes: regular potatoes, sweet potatoes, and turnips

- Spices: garlic, thyme, oregano, rosemary, basil, mint, cinnamon, and pepper

- Fish: salmon, tuna, white fish, sardines, trout, oysters, mussels, shrimp, etc.

- Olive oil: extra virgin olive oil is mainly used for frying and as a basis for a dressing

If you have known my website for a while, you know that these are all healthy products. Potatoes can still be argued, of course, but the combination of all the above products is very healthy. Then once in a while, a potato can't hurt either.

Which products you can eat in moderation

Then there are products that you should eat in moderation. The majority of your diet should, therefore, consist of the basic products, and you can supplement them with the following products:

• Poultry: chicken, turkey, quail, and duck

• Eggs: from all the above animals

• Cheese: mozzarella, blue cheese, brie, and Parmesan cheese

• Dairy products: milk, buttermilk, and Greek yogurt

These are, of course, all animal products. They aren't a big fan of the Mediterranean diet, but they are a great addition to the basic products.

Which Products You Can Eat From Time To Time

Very occasionally, it is permitted to eat red meat.

Although the majority of red meat is unprocessed, it is less healthy. Red meat can develop the risk of cancer and a heart attack.

That is why you should only eat this type of meat very occasionally. In addition, unprocessed red meat is generally more expensive than poultry or fish. That, too, is probably a reason why it was not eaten much in those areas.

Red meat includes:

• Beef: beef steaks, different types of steaks and organ meats

• Pork: pork tenderloin, pork chops, and fillet steaks

• Lamb: lamb legs, rack of lamb, and shoulder chop

Which products you should avoid

And unfortunately, I'm not done yet. You now know precisely what you can eat. But also in diet, there is a category of products that you should avoid at all times.

The following products are not in the diet:

• Added sugar products: all soft drinks, fruit juices, candy, pasta, cookies, and ice cream.

• Refined grain products: white bread, white pasta, and all other fast-absorbing carbohydrate sources.

• Trans fats: these unuseful fats are found in many processed products such as cakes, pasta, ready meals, but also in margarine and low-fat margarine.

• Processed meat: hot dogs, sausages, sausage rolls, spare ribs, hamburgers, salami, sandwich sausage, liver sausage, etc.

• Highly processed foods: you should think of products that come from the factory. Also, products with light reduced-fat or lean on it.

As you may have already noticed, all the products that you should avoid are processed products. Not one of these products grows on a tree, or you can pick them from nature.

What can you drink with the Mediterranean diet?

What probably does not come as a surprise is that mainly water is drunk in these areas. This is also an essential drink in this diet. It is wise to always have this with you so that you get enough fluid during the day.

The Mediterranean diet contains moderate amounts of red wine - think of 1 glass per day. However, this is entirely optional. Red wine contains resveratrol, which is one of the few alcoholic drinks that still has certain benefits.

If you have a predisposition for alcohol addiction, then this snack is not wise. But you probably expected that yourself.

You can also drink black coffee and especially green tea in this diet. However, no sugar may be added here.

All drinks with added sugar are strictly prohibited according to this diet. And also, fresh fruit juices are discouraged by a large number of sugars. After all, you only squeeze the moisture and sugars from the fruit. Unfortunately, the fibers remain behind, which means that these drinks are also unhealthy.

Not all Mediterranean diets are the same

The Mediterranean area consists of different countries around the Mediterranean Sea. Not all eating habits are, therefore, the same. But it is not only the countries that differ in the Mediterranean diet.

A large study also showed that the level of education and income determine the quality of the Mediterranean diet.

Eighteen thousand adherents of the Mediterranean diet were studied in this study. They discovered that when people followed this diet, the risk of cardiovascular disease only decreased in people who had higher education levels and/or had more income. The researchers saw no benefits for those who had completed primary education and had a lower income.

That may sound silly, but those are the results of this study.

How does this work exactly?

The Mediterranean diet that emphasizes products such as olive oil, fish, nuts, seeds, and legumes lowers the risk of many lifestyle diseases. And yet, there were different results between different classes of life.

The groups had to adhere to an optimal Mediterranean diet. This was measured by a score they received from the intake of different products from the following product groups:

- Fruit

- regards

- Nuts

- Legumes

- Cereals

- Fish

- Fats

- Meat

People with a higher socioeconomic position (higher income or higher level of education) generally showed more favorable eating habits.

The people who experienced the health effects of this diet had a diet richer in antioxidants (polyphenols), as well as whole-grain products, organic foods, and a variety of fruits and vegetables.

In other words: not all Mediterranean diets are the same. The diet determines which product groups you eat, but not the quality of these products.

Think of nuts, seeds, and legumes. Walnuts are extremely expensive compared to peanuts:

- The kilo price of walnuts at the Albert Heijn costs: 13.95 euros

- The kilo price of peanuts at the Albert Heijn costs: 2.70 euros

Walnuts may be much more expensive, but they are also many times healthier for the human body. Peanuts can hardly be called healthy for the body. The difference in health is due to the omega 3/6 ratio that contains walnuts and peanuts.

The more qualitative your products are, the more health benefits you will experience.

The Benefits ofthe Mediterranean Diet

If you follow the Mediterranean diet and especially eat quality products, then this diet can have many health benefits. Below I list the five most important benefits.

Benefit # 1: the diet is ideal for weight loss

That the Mediterranean diet is healthy has been proven.

Good health starts with a healthy weight. The Mediterranean diet can certainly help you on your way.

This type of diet makes it possible to lose weight without being hungry. You can get the weight off in a realistic way and last a lifetime.

• The diet is sustainable. You'd better say it's not a diet; it's a lifestyle.

• There is room for many different diet forms within this diet. Whether you prefer low carbohydrate, less protein, or somewhere in between, everything is possible:

• The intake of high-quality protein-rich foods is essential within this diet. You need to get the proteins from poultry, legumes, and other healthy products.

• The quality of your carbohydrates goes up drastically. Instead of refined carbohydrates, only whole-grain carbs are permitted to a limited extent. For the rest, you supplement your carbohydrate requirement with vegetables, fruit, beans, and nuts.

If you follow the diet in this way, you have the opportunity to lose weight in a healthy way.

For example, there is a study in which three different diets were tested — the low-carb, low-fat, and Mediterranean diet.

In this study, the low carbohydrate group lost the most weight with 5.5 kilograms. The group that followed the Mediterranean diet lost an average of 4.6 kilograms. And last but not least, the low-fat group lost 3.3 kilograms.

Advantage # 2: it reduces the risk of type 2 diabetes

Type 2 diabetes, poor cholesterol levels, overweight, and cardiovascular diseases are all conditions in which a poor lifestyle plays a significant role.

If you have an unhealthy lifestyle, the chance of developing all the above disorders is, therefore, very high.

But let's start with type 2 diabetes.

You develop diabetes type 2 because you bombard your body with carbohydrates and sugars for a long time. And that is especially about fast carbohydrates and sugars. What is included?

- Refined grains (white bread, white pasta, cruesli, cornflakes, and most other pasta)

- Sweets

- Cakes

- White rice

- Soft drinks/fruit juices

The above products are certainly part of the Western diet. And that is precisely the reason why type 2 diabetes is so prevalent in the Netherlands and other Western countries.

If you bombard your body so often and with the above products, your body must produce extremely much insulin to be able to process this. Your body will eventually become insensitive to insulin, which means that more and more insulin is needed to be able to handle the sugars until you arrive at a point where the body no longer responds to this or even produces insulin.

And then you are "blessed" with type 2 diabetes.

To prevent this, it is essential that you mainly eat products that have little or no influence on your blood sugar level. The Mediterranean diet recommends mostly unprocessed products from nature.

Products such as legumes, vegetables, fruit, nuts, beans, and seeds are products that are high in fiber and therefore have a much lower effect on your blood sugar levels. For this reason alone, it reduces the risk of developing type 2 diabetes by 52%.

Advantage # 3: it reduces the risk of cardiovascular disease

The development of cardiovascular diseases often does not happen without a struggle.

There are often many problems beforehand:

- You develop overweight

- Your cholesterol levels deteriorate

- You become insulin resistant and then becomes type 2 diabetes

- You develop high blood pressure

Coincidentally, these are all risk factors for the development of cardiovascular disease. In tip three, you learned that you acquire the above disorders mainly because of an unhealthy lifestyle.

How can the Mediterranean diet reduce the risk of cardiovascular disease?

Research shows that following the Mediterranean diet, including eating many monounsaturated fats and omega-3 foods, is associated with a significant reduction in death from all sorts of causes, but especially heart disease.

For example, the Mediterranean diet is rich in olive oil. Olive oil contains alpha-linolenic acid (ALA), and this substance reduces the risk of a heart attack. Research has shown that the Mediterranean diet reduced the risk of a heart attack by 30%.

But this is, of course, not only due to olive oil (although this is a big part of the diet). The diet generally uses very healthy nutrients that already significantly reduce the risk of all risk factors.

Advantage # 4: it reduces the chance of cognitive diseases

The Mediterranean diet is rich in healthy products. And so also with healthy fats.

In general, it is recommended to eat fatty fish (which contains a lot of omega-3 fatty acids) at least twice a week and to eat a lot of olive oil and nuts.

All these products are healthy for the body because of the fats. For example, fats play an important role in the brain.

Seventy-seven percent of our brains are water. When we remove all that water, the dry weight of the brain remains. Of this dry weight, our brains appear to consist of no less than 60% fat. Our brain is, therefore, a fat organ.

What is not so strange is to think that fatty acids play an essential role in our brains. And that is also true:

Fatty acids play a huge role in the construction and maintenance of the brain.

And especially omega-3 fatty acids help with this.

Benefit # 5: it helps to fight cancer

Vegetable food, especially fruit and vegetables, is the cornerstone of the Mediterranean diet.

Plants generally contain many antioxidants:

These are slightly toxic substances that the plant has to combat insects. This actually ensures that a plant can last longer.

Antioxidants give bright colors to fruit and generally give a bitter taste to vegetables. That is also why it scares off insects. Very handy.

Antioxidants are not only useful for the plants themselves, but they are also very healthy for our bodies. Antioxidants ensure that your body becomes better at cleaning up broken cells, inflammations, and tumors. In addition, the Mediterranean diet has a balanced ratio of omega-3 and omega-6 fatty acids. This is also conducive to cancer prevention.

The Mediterranean diet is characterized by a lot of unprocessed food and a lot of extra virgin olive oil. It has generally been found that cancer is much less common in these areas than in Western countries. Southern Europeans, therefore, have a lower risk of cancer, and scientists believe that olive oil has something to do with this.

Cancer is basically caused by uncontrolled cell growth in our body. This uncontrolled cell growth can occur due to damage to a body cell. The antioxidants in olive oil can limit the damage of these by reacting with free radicals.

As a result, these free radicals can no longer cause damage to our bodies.

And what about the disadvantages exactly?

Every diet has disadvantages. But I have to admit that I can hardly name any difficulties with the Mediterranean diet.

As I've always indicated, unprocessed food is the healthiest and most natural for your body. After all, it is how we ate (mainly) in prehistoric times. It is, therefore, not surprising that this is the healthiest way to grow old and stay healthy.

What is a disadvantage for some people?

The diet can be reasonably priced. It is expected that you eat fish twice a week that you eat a lot of fruit and vegetables. And nuts and seeds are also not cheap products.

I must honestly say that I personally think this kind of disadvantage is nonsense since good health is priceless. And you will undoubtedly get good health from the Mediterranean diet.

Experiences of people who have followed the diet

- You lose weight

- It is a way of life and not a diet

- You feel less tired and lifeless

- You are not hungry

- You can eat very varied food

- Losing weight is difficult

- It takes a lot of discipline to keep cooking the Mediterranean

Recipes from the Mediterranean diet

Breakfast recipe # 1: healthy yogurt breakfast

Ingredients:

- 150 ml semi-skimmed yogurt

- 40 grams of fresh muesli without added sugar   Granola

- 20 grams of mixed nuts

- One large tablespoon of blueberries

Preparation:

Put the yogurt inside a bowl and mix in all the ingredients.

Lunch recipe # 2: Tuna salad

Ingredients:

3/4 cup

100 grams of new potatoes

30 grams of arugula

One tablespoon olive oil

Half a bowl of mushrooms, cut into thin slices

One can of tuna

, dip

One tablespoon tapenade of green olives

30 grams of black olives, pitted

Preparation:

Halve the fresh potatoes, and then cook them in plenty of water with a little salt for 10 minutes. Allow cooling afterward.

Heat up the oil inside a frying pan and fry the mushrooms for 2 minutes on high heat.

Drain the tuna and collect the oil. Mix the tuna oil with the tapenade. Mix the tuna in a bowl with the new potatoes, mushrooms, and olives.

Gently stir the tapenade dressing into the salad. Mix in the arugula at the end.

Dinner recipe # 3: a Mediterranean chicken dish with olives

Ingredients:

Two tablespoons olive oil

Two onions, sliced

Two cloves of garlic, crushed

One tablespoon rosemary

Two large peppers

1 . 4 0 2

40 grams of sun-dried tomatoes

400 grams of canned tomato cubes · 2 Cups

Three tablespoons white wine

Four chicken chops, skinned and boneless

50 grams of olives, pitted

1. 7 02

Preparation:

Heat up the olive oil inside a large frying pan or deep frying pan and fry the onion with rosemary over medium heat for 5 minutes until the onion is lightly colored. Add to this regularly.

Add the bell pepper and fry for a few minutes over medium heat. Keep remapping regularly.

Add the sun-dried tomatoes and canned tomatoes with liquid. Pour in the wine. Season with freshly ground black pepper and salt, mix the mixture and bring to a boil.

Stir the chicken pieces into the sauce. Bring it back to the boil and turn the heat down. Let the stew simmer covered for 25-30 minutes until the chicken and vegetables are tender.

Stir in the olives shortly before serving.

Health effects

A study conducted on a sample of 22,000 people showed that adherence to the Mediterranean diet, compared with the traditional American diet, and reduces the risk of heart disease and by 24% of cancer by 33%. Multiple medical studies have shown that residents of the Mediterranean countries are less at risk of cardiovascular disease, less likely to suffer from overweight, high blood pressure, and diabetes. A Mediterranean diet does reduce the risk of Alzheimer's disease. This is due primarily to the abundant consumption of fresh vegetables and fruits, dishes from cereals, and a moderate amount of meat and fish (fats enter the body mainly from olive oil).

Scientists from the University of Rovira and Virgili conducted studies in which they concluded that the Mediterranean diet, combined with exercise, helps to reduce weight over the year by at least five percent of the original body weight, improve glucose uptake and maintain positive dynamics over time. The study involved over 600 patients aged 55 to 75 years, suffering from obesity or overweight, as well as metabolic syndrome.

Attempts were regularly made to isolate the components of the diet that give such a strong medical effect, and fatty fish, seafood, olive oil, red wine, etc. were declared as such, but systematic studies have shown that it is impossible to isolate one or two separate components, despite their indeed a positive effect.

The World Health Organization has published nutritional recommendations for a proven reduction in the risk of cardiovascular disease, many of which overlap with the traditional Mediterranean diet:

• It is recommended to avoid eating foods with cholesterol, such as "red" animal meat, in favor of fish, seafood, chicken, and pasta;

• It is recommended to avoid foods containing fatty acids that stimulate the generation of cholesterol by the human body itself, such as cream, butter, lard, in favor of olive or sunflower oil;

• It is recommended to eat about five servings of fruits and vegetables per day, as well as dishes with maximum preservation of plant fibers, both whole and in salads;

• Reduce the use of sweets in favor of fruits;

• Eat at least one time per week dishes from oily fish for eating from it omega-3 acid that destroys cholesterol;

• Do not use dishes with a lot of salt;

• Diet is combined with an active lifestyle.

Typical Products

• Olive oil and olives

• Fresh vegetables: tomatoes, eggplant, bell pepper, zucchini

• Garlic, onion

• Fish and seafood

- Greens, for example, thyme, rosemary, oregano, and basil

- White bread, pasta, and rice

- In some countries, regular consumption of red wine

Power balance:

- 60% carbohydrates (bread, pasta, fruits, vegetables)

- 30% fat (mainly olive oil)

- 10% protein (meat, fish, beans, peas, beans)

Mediterranean diet for weight loss

The Mediterranean diet is essentially a balanced, healthy diet. According to nutritionists, it has no contraindications and is not harmful to health.

The benefits of the Mediterranean diet

An essential plus of this diet is the absence of contraindications. The menu is balanced, it contains all the substances necessary for the body, and therefore it is not forbidden to people with diseases, pregnant women, lactating women, and even teenagers. Do not go on a diet only in case of allergies and individual intolerance to products.

Most of the diet consists of fruits, vegetables, vegetable fats, and proteins, and sweets and fatty meat are removed. The slow process of losing weight goes on its own without a feeling of hunger and stress due to the consumption of low-calorie, wholesome foods and the exclusion of harmful foods. It is additionally recommended to engage in all possible sports.

Cons of the Mediterranean Diet

The main minus of the diet - it helps to lose weight extremely slowly. Its main goal is to become accustomed to a healthy diet and improve health. Excess weight will go away very slowly, and with severe obesity, the result can be expected for quite some time.

However, on such a diet, you can live and eat so consistently with the benefit of organisms, unlike many other diets. Gradually, metabolic problems will even out, and the weight will return to normal; you need to be patient.

It will also be difficult for those accustomed to sweeten tea and eat cakes to unlearn it sharply since sweets are prohibited during the diet. We advise you to do this gradually, reducing the daily dose of sugar a little - then there will be no temptation to break, and the stress from stopping the usual dose of sugar will be minimized.

Weekly Menu for Mediterranean Diet

The menu is characterized by a large number of low-fat fish and seafood, 4-6 times a week. Fish is replaced by the usual fried meatballs and pork, which are banned. Lean beef, chicken, turkey, and rabbit can be eaten. The number of dairy products without additives with low percentages of fat is also increasing. Dairy products and fruits can be eaten every day, but only unsweetened.

Simple carbohydrates - sweets, sugar, are replaced with complex ones: pasta from whole grain cereals, coarse bread, cereals. Fatty hard cheeses are replaced with low-fat - mozzarella, curd.

Potatoes and sweet fruits like bananas need to be very limited — alcohol, fatty, spicy, banned. You can only dry wine no more than a glass a day.

Results

As a result of the diet, a very smooth weight loss occurs without the slightest harm to the body, and the kilograms left do not return immediately after the diet is terminated since the body did not experience stress. However, it will not work to achieve special weight loss since the diet does not limit the diet, but rather is the basis for a rational, healthy diet. For a week, a loss of up to 3 kg is possible.

The Mediterranean diet can be used to transition to a constantly balanced diet gradually.

Nutritionist reviews

- The Mediterranean diet is not much like a diet in the usual sense. This is not a strict restriction of products and a reduction in diet, but fractional, nutritious nutrition. One of the few diets that do not have special restrictions is even suitable for constant nutrition. Just don't wait for a quick result, but it will be stable, and without harm to health, "says Dilara Akhmetova, nutritionist consultant, nutrition coach.

Preparing meals in advance is a practice designed to cook, during a single day, dishes that last for the rest of the week. It is a good way to save time and eat healthily. Developing a routine of planning, shopping, and preparation will help you minimize the boredom generated by eating the same dishes and improving your health.

Go shopping

• Choose a day of the week to go grocery shopping. Schedule a schedule and complete it every week. Many people buy Saturdays or Sundays and prepare their meals on Sunday.

• Save your favorite recipes. Although you can make your meals without following official recipes, it is advisable to do so if you enjoy stews, pasta, dishes that are prepared in the slow cooker, or soups.

• Categorize your recipes in a folder according to the main ingredients. That way, you can choose several dishes that require the same protein, vegetable, or whole grain.

• Make a list. Take your folder and identify the ingredients you need to use for the week, like the chicken or pumpkin. Get a list of all the ingredients you required, so you do not buy on impulse.

• Wholesale purchase. If you do not have a store membership, you may want to try it. Preparing meals in advance and buying in bulk are two practices that complement each other because you cook large portions in a single day to use them all week.

• Try using this test shopping list. It should include two main proteins, three to five vegetables, two to three whole grains, and other ingredients. The following is a test list:

• Dairy products: low-fat feta cheese, parmesan cheese, Greek yogurt, and low-fat mozzarella cheese

- Packaged or bulk products: black beans, chickpeas, corn, wholemeal bread, pasta sauce, vegetable broth, quinoa or couscous

- Fruits and vegetables: basil, red peppers, a head of broccoli, a pint of tomatoes, a head of garlic, a head of lettuce, lemon, parsley, two onions, potatoes, and strawberries

- Protein: chicken breast, eggs, prawns, ground beef or sausages

- Spices and oil: Use olive or coconut oil, spices, vinegar, mayonnaise, aluminum foil, or butter paper.

Preparation

Start the morning preparation day. Keep in mind that spending a whole day in the kitchen will reduce or completely eliminate the amount of time you will use to cook during the week. Most people do it on Sundays or Mondays.

Prepare a big breakfast with pancakes or waffles. Double or triple the usual amount, so you can eat them a couple of days a week. Preparing a large bowl of dough is cheap, but these foods can make you feel more decadent than a bowl of cereal.

• Try preparing protein pancakes; they are healthier.

• Replace the waffles and pancakes with a large batch of breakfast burritos. Stir a couple of eggs, prepare some sausages and add cheese and beans.

• Freeze them and each morning heat one in the microwave oven.

• Prepare a stew, pasta sauce, or chicken dish in the slow cooker. Schedule it for 6 or 8 hours. It will be your lunch or dinner to reheat during the week.

• Boil some eggs. Eggs are ideal as snacks, but they can also be added to salads or eaten during breakfast to increase protein intake.

• Chicken or turkey handle. Remove the skin of two or four breasts and place them under the broiler for 6 to 10 minutes on each side. Place a little water in a saucepan under the grate so that the chicken is juicier.

• Prepare the most complicated recipe for dinner on Sunday night. Double the recipe so you have leftovers for the rest of the week.

• Bakes buns or bars. They last all week and can be as healthy as you decide. They are versatile and could be served for breakfast, as sandwiches, or as a dessert.

• Prepare a large batch of brown rice, quinoa, couscous, or wild rice. Cook at least four cups. Prepare a different grain each week to obtain different nutrients.

• Sauté, roast, or steam your vegetables. Use butter, coconut oil, or olive oil and season with salt and pepper. Mix them to reduce the preparation time.

• Slice chicken, vegetables, and fruits. Place them in large stacks on the sideboard no more than 30 minutes before packing them.

Packaging

Buy a large package of Tupperware style containers and freezer packaging. You need enough meals for five days, so make sure you have at least 15 large containers and some extra for rooms or accompaniments. Make sure they are suitable for the microwave oven.

•   Save the leftovers from Sunday's dinner in two freezer containers. Remove them from the freezer one night before serving them so that they thaw in the fridge. This reduces the risk of food spoiling because, if necessary, you can keep more than a week in the freezer.

•   Pack your breakfasts Pack breakfast burritos or portions of pancakes and place them in the fridge or freezer. Separate 115 g (4 oz) of yogurt from a large package and add a little fruit on top.

•   Mix fruit and yogurt to prepare a fruit salad. Place it in 5 to 10 individual containers to serve during breakfast, lunch, as a snack, or for dinner.

• Prepare lunch packages. Place half a cup of rice or other grain in the bottom of the bowl. Add 115 to 230 g (4 to 6 oz) of sliced chicken breast and a cup of assorted vegetables.

• Fill a small container with your favorite sauce and, with adhesive tape, attach it to each package to add it to your lunch after heating it.

• Replace the grain with spinach or lettuce and prepare a salad for your lunch.

• Place bakery and confectionery products in airtight containers. If you bake too many and you will not consume them that same week, freeze some for the next one.

• Place the vegetables, protein, and grains that you will use for another recipe in individual containers. If you are preparing fast salads, pasta, or tacos for dinner, you can add those ready-made foods before preparing or serving them.

• Organize your fridge. Place containers with breakfast in one area, lunch in another, and dinner in another. Label them as necessary or organize your containers by color.

• Place anything you do not want to eat in the next three days in the freezer. You can thaw it later. This is especially important if it involves chicken, fish, or unsalted pork.

Healthy Eating

Healthy Diet Recommendations

Of course, the ideal human diet composition depends on the type of activity, lifestyle, and place of residence. Still, there are more or less universal tips developed by health organizations:

• Carefully monitor the calorie content of the products and body weight. So, the State Research Center for Preventive Medicine (GNITsPM) recommends reducing excess weight with a body mass index higher than 27 kg / m.

• Limit your energy intake from fats. Saturated fats (animals, solid vegetable fats) - should be up to 1/3 of the consumed fats; the remaining 2/3 of the fats should be unsaturated, liquid fats. When consuming milk and dairy products, preference should be given to products with reduced fat content. Try not to eat foods containing trans fatty acids.

- Strive to increase the proportion of fruits, vegetables, whole grains, legumes, and nuts in your daily diet. It is from this food that 50-60% of all energy should be obtained.

- About a third of bread, cereals, flour right in the diet should be foods enriched with micronutrients.

- Limit the intake of simple carbohydrates (sugar, honey, sweet carbonated drinks) - no more than 30-40 g per day.

- Limit your salt intake and consume only the iodized salt.

- Try to provide the body system with vitamins in physiological quantities, including antioxidants (vitamins A, C, E), folic acid. If your diet doesn't really include sufficient vitamins from the food, you can periodically take multivitamins and optionally vitamin D.

- Consult a doctor on diet topics, trust only nutrition developed by reputable healthcare institutions.

Research History

The first full-scale study to confirm that a healthy diet can significantly reduce problems with cardiovascular disease, obesity, and diabetes was the North Karelia project, which was launched in Finland in 1973. Over 35 years, the mortality from cardiovascular diseases among the population of the region of North Karelia decreased by seven times. This result formed the basis of the Pan-European Health Strategy 2020.

The main changes that led the North Karelia project to this result:

1.   Quit smoking

2.   Change in diet:

•   80% reduction in butter consumption;

•   Increased consumption of vegetable oil;

- Consumption of low-fat dairy products;

- Increased consumption of fruits and vegetables;

- Changing recipes for traditional dishes and teaching the population new cooking techniques (not frying, but baking and boiling).

What Is A Healthy Meal?

A healthy meal contains a lot of vegetables. So most of the plate should consist of vegetables such as zucchini, cucumber, peppers, or other vegetables; this guarantees a lot of vitamins, low calories, and a nice freshness (if the vegetables are not overcooked).

Colorful

Of course, it is not enough just to eat vegetables; it should also be varied and colorful. Ideally, the vegetables are as mixed and colorful as a traffic light: yellow, red, and green. A white vegetable such as white cabbage and cauliflower is not wrong and serves as a colorful icing on the cake. The colorful mixture, which changes repeatedly, also offers many vitamins and a varied taste. Even if you love something (such as tomatoes), it's important to vary a bit. Otherwise, deficiency symptoms can occur, and the food becomes boring over time.

Protein

Protein is one of the essential components of our body. However, not as much as needed, as many believe. And even then, it does not always have to be animal protein. Other sources of Protein from beans and tofu provide a change in the daily diet and bring creativity to life.

Carbohydrates

Again and again, the diets with "low-carb" (pronounced the "little-carbohydrates") the total hit. No wonder. Carbohydrates also make you fat. At least if you eat too many of them, if you eat them in the wrong combination (i.e., with too much fat or sugar) or do not vary enough. Carbohydrates are generally crucial in order for us to have energy, an essential ingredient for satiety, and it's important because it's good for your nerves, among other things.

Of course

The best thing you can do for your body is to win food from natural ingredients. Fruits and vegetables are, at best, varieties that are available regionally and seasonally. Of course, it is okay from time to time sometimes not to eat regional specialties, such as pineapple or bananas (if you live in Germany, there will probably be hardly regional), but it is completely superfluous outside the strawberry time overpriced strawberries from Africa to buy, which taste like nothing and have hardly any vitamins.

The five no-gos:

1. a lot of fat

Fat is good for the body. If we have too little fat, it will harm our health in the long run. But many people have the problem of eating too much fat, which is not healthy either. Obesity is a modern disease that can easily turn into obesity. Too much fat is bad for the brain, the immune system, and the arteries, which in turn can cause a heart attack.

Of course, one must distinguish between healthy fats (olive oil, nut oil, nuts) and unhealthy fats (butter, animal fats, etc.) because fat is not the same fat.

Lots of sugar

it is perfectly okay to consume sugar. Because sugar is an energy supplier, and sugar tastes good too. However, much sugar isn't good for the body and the immune system and can lead to addiction, particularly in bad cases. Above all, sugar has the disadvantage that it does not fill you up for long and that you quickly lose energy again. Even if you are pushed by sugar, the effect lasts only very briefly.

Chemical substances

Our body is a natural organism; it does not need any chemical additives, so why should you forcefully pump yourself with chemistry? Unfortunately, many people tend to stuff themselves with ready-made sauce-fix bags and other unhealthy things for convenience. It may not be a problem to feed a little unhealthy; you will not die because you incorporate some e-substance. However, too many chemical foods are not good for your health. This can cause many other diseases of affluence that you would not normally have.

Many spices

People like spicy food, and that's perfectly fine, but certain levels of spiciness and too much salt are not among the spices people need on the contrary. The man needs a little salt. In fact, pretty much all foods contain some salt naturally, and the over-flavoring of food causes water retention, is bad for the brain and has a negative effect on the organism.

One-sided

The worst you can do to yourself and your body is to eat one-sidedly. It does not matter whether the food bathes in fat, whether you are constantly fed on peppers, eating too much sugar or too little Fruit, any form of one-sided diet has the result that you have deficiency symptoms, and you get sick sooner or later becomes. This can be in a one-sided diet, where you eat only unhealthy things, and in a one-sided diet in which you eat only healthy food because one-sided is and remains one-sided. That cannot and should not be the goal because ironing out these deficiencies requires a lot of work and a lot of discipline.

What are macros?

Macros or macronutrients are the nutrients of the diet, i.e., Protein, carbohydrates, and lipids. They are the ones who will generate energy.

They are opposed to micronutrients that they have no energy value and the body in minute amounts. In other words, it is vitamins, minerals, and trace elements. However, do not get me wrong; the body absolutely needs it.

Macros: Carbohydrates, Proteins & Lipids

Carbohydrates

These are sugars and carbohydrates. It is the Carbohydrates that will be the primary source of energy for your body and especially your brain. It can be cereals (rice, corn, and wheat), legumes (red beans, chickpeas, and lentils), fast sugar (sucrose), Fruit (fructose), etc.

They divide two types:

- Fast sugars (foods with sweet tastes) and, therefore, directly assimilated by the body.

- Slow sugars (since they have more gradual assimilation, as the name suggests).

The Proteins

The essential element of our muscles, skin, enzymes, hormones, antibodies proteins consists of amino acids. That's why we are often told that proteins build our muscles! And those amino acids, such as BCAA, come to repair our small muscles after a good training session.

Unlike carbohydrates or lipids, proteins cannot be stored by the body: it must, therefore, be brought daily.

Lipids or "fats."

Lipids are the structure of the membranes of our cells. They also participate in the transport of proteins for the development of some of our essential hormones; finally, they serve as vehicles for specific vitamins.

Lipids must necessarily be brought by food because our body does not know how to make them.

The good fats: our body is ABSOLUTELY necessary; they are found in particular in the fish. The dried Fruit, lawyers, and some oils are also sources of lipids unusual, but to consume moderately.

The bad fats are usually found in processed foods: pastries, fries, burgers, sweets, but also in cheese and butter.

Basic rules

Bring carbohydrates, fats, and proteins to your body every day. Stop the sugar fast. It is hiding anywhere, and you will have to track it down!!! For this, turn to the least processed foods possible, learn to read labels, and put in place processes to get you out of this addiction.

Consume fruits but limit the daily amount.

Do not remove fats: consume in the right quantity (see below) every day; good fats are to be preferred.

This is why you should never copy the diets of other individuals, but rather strive to create your own nutritional plan by following the basic rules mentioned above and according to your objectives.

In general, here is the good distribution:

• CARBOHYDRATES: 55% of the total caloric intake

• PROTEIN: 30% of total caloric intake

• LIPID: 15% of the total calorie intake.

And if you just want to have a good diet without worrying about making a dry or mass gain: I also have to count my macros?

In this case, just calculate the number of calories needed on a day.

And then divide between carbohydrates, proteins, and lipids according to the ratios mentioned above.

Keeping in mind that:

•   1g of Carbohydrates provides four calories,

•   1 g Protein provides four calories.

•   1 g of fat provides nine calories.

And that one should not generally exceed 1.2g of Protein per kg of ideal weight in the woman and 1.5 kg of protein perk in the man.

How to Store and Reheat Your Meals

Do you like to shop for a long time, and when you come back from the supermarket it's not to go back two days later? It is more practical, obviously! We still need to keep the food that we buy and avoid surprises. There are many different methods and tips from the fridge to the cellophane to keep your dishes longer. To know them, look! A video signed E = M6.

Keeping a cooked dish when the dish you have prepared so well is still in large quantities, you only want one thing: keep it.

To do this:

- They must be put in aluminum trays

- They must be packed in containers with hermetic lids

- The trays must support the freezing and the microwave oven

You can keep a cooked dish for up to 48 hours. After that, it becomes unfit for consumption because of bacteria. In this case, it is strongly recommended to place it in the freezer. It can be enjoyed one year later in some cases. But there are, of course, some other kinds of food preservation, as explained by Mac Leggy in his E = M6 show.

Dehydration storage Dehydration removes water from food. Water is indeed conducive to the multiplication of bacteria, yeasts, and molds. The technique of air drying this process is rather industrial. It eliminates the water contained in food.

This is the case for:

- Cereals

- Figs

- Rusks and biscuits

- Green beans

- Peppers

- Etc.

The smoking technique in this conservation technique, the food is exposed to wood smoke. Smoking is frequently combined with salting or drying. Smoking is used for the preservation of:

- Fish

- Bacon

- Ham

Salting is a technique that involves soaking food with sodium chloride. In other words, the dishes are impregnated with salt. The water is unavailable and allows keeping the dish longer:

- Herring

- Sausages

- Anchovies

Acidification, The vast majority of microbes cannot grow in the presence of certain acids. Acidification makes it possible to keep the dish longer, hence the conservation of gherkins and yogurts longer.

Art And / Or Technique to Warm Up Your Dishes

One of the conditions for a dish to be appetizing is that it is not dehydrated. When cooked for the first time, some of its natural water evaporated. To find a tantalizing aspect during its reheating, it will have to bring a dose of moisture in parallel.

If you use the microwave

This is the fastest way to warm your dishes. The microwave principle is based on the agitation of the molecules of food, which causes its warming and a loss of water. It is advised is to place a glass of water (cold) next to your dish to generate steam. You will see, your gratin will find a beautiful appearance and softness.

Focus on potatoes (including French fries)

While we can always warm his potatoes in the microwave, but it is not the ideal tool. If you still have fries or fried potatoes, it is best to return them to the pan with a little oil over medium heat. Spread your fries or pans well and make several batches if necessary.

Reheat rice or Pasta

Rice and Pasta tend to dry out during storage. To warm them up and find them soft, the ideal is to use a steamer or use a pan with a bottom of the water.

How to make your next trip at the grocery store fast and simple

The grocery store, a weekly ritual

Doing groceries, groceries, the market, shopping... No matter how you think it, it remains an essential activity well anchored in families' everyday lives. Canadians do spend about 62 hours a year buying food, according to a study on grocery consumption. Their ritual is to go there once a week, especially on Saturdays, to stay on average one hour for a $ 140 bill. Some people prefer to shop from day to day, as needed.

Whether you are one or the other, you have surely noticed that your bill is more and saltier. In fact, in 2014, the grocery basket price of Canadians increased by 2.2% compared to the previous year.

Although it can be very easy to walk the cart from one row to another, catching a few items here and there, you will find that it does not take much to explode its budget. All the temptations are there, but it is up to you to adopt some habits to avoid catches in the supermarket. Therefore, we have prepared a guide to advise that will do well both for your wallet and your health!

Five habits to take before going to the supermarket

Do you know that it is possible to save money even before going to the grocery store? All you need is good planning, a grocery list in hand, and a budget in mind for a winning grocery store! Here are some habits to adopt before going to the grocery store.

Follow a list that you will respect.

Going shopping without having a grocery list is like going on a trip without a road map. Your list is your precious tool and your benchmark to avoid oversights and unnecessary purchases.

Plan your visit to the supermarket

It is important to plan when you will go shopping. Ideally, put your calendar on one date per week. If you go there more frequently, you will expose yourself to unnecessary purchases.

Like road traffic, there are rush hours in grocery stores. The worst moments are after work hours and weekend afternoons. If you can, do your shopping while the store is not too busy. Studies show that most consumers buy more when the store is full.

One of the best things to do is know when your grocery store is starting its promotions to plan your tour. It is generally Wednesday that new sales are displayed in Quebec and Ontario, while for Western Canada, it is Friday.

Remember to do your shopping in the morning, because it is often a quiet moment of the day when fresh products (fruits, vegetables, meat, etc.) have just been placed on the shelves, and the shelves are filled.

Otherwise, grocery shopping in the evening also has its advantages. The aisles will not be crowded, and you will have a full stomach, so less risk for impulsive purchases.

Set a budget

Above all, it is essential to develop a food budget according to your means and your needs. By setting a weekly amount, it will become easier to identify if you meet your goals. Plus, this is a very effective strategy for saving!

Read the circulars

Would you be that surprised to know that flyers do not necessarily have discounted products? Indeed, balances usually appear on the first and last pages. Others are promoting items that can make us believe they are cheaper.

Also, take advantage of circular deals to try new products. Your meals and snacks can sometimes seem redundant over time. So, why not give yourself a little challenge by trying a new fruit or vegetable a month or a week?

Use coupons smartly

Couponing is very trendy today. You'll find discounts in newspapers, magazines, the Internet, mobile apps, and more.

However, do not fall into such a trap of coupons. They save money and are very beneficial to the extent that you use them for items you really need. Just because you have a coupon for such a product does not mean you have to buy it.

Some grocery stores also offer reward cards that may encourage us to purchase key products that give more "points." Be careful and respect your grocery list!

Good Things to Save At the Supermarket

If you are thinking of buying some foods, opt for a small basket. A big cart will make you fill it. Choose it according to your needs!

Circulate clockwise

Did you know that the location of a grocery store entrance can have a significant effect on the way you shop? Access on the right will make you circulate counterclockwise. Studies show that consumers who travel in this direction spend, on average, $2 more than consumers who travel clockwise. Conversely, a door on the left will move you in the right direction, and you will save!

This is because customers who go to the left tend to focus more forward and less backward. They spend less time there, so fewer expenses. By placing the door on the right, grocery stores have noticed that they are doing better deals than those having access to the center or left.

The next time you go to the grocery store, turn left immediately to save a few dollars! Of course, not all grocery stores are built that way.

Do your shopping in U

Start your market in the fresh produce section and do the U: all the essential commodities are there, such as fruits and vegetables, dairy products, meat, etc. If you start with the purchase of basic items, you will not have much room for unnecessary food in the center aisles.

Moreover, the most common way to get around the supermarket is to do the perimeter while browsing the different shelves, as needed.

Stick to the main aisles

In Canada, 71% of consumers walk all the aisles to make sure they do not forget anything. However, this is a waste of time and an obstacle to your savings. By performing each of the aisles, you will succumb to the temptation of commodities you do not need. Make a habit of visiting only the main ones, especially those on the outskirts.

Consider ugly foods

You will see more and more in Canadian supermarkets of deformed fruits and vegetables that are often ignored by consumers. Know that these small fruits and imperfect vegetables are sold 30% cheaper than those that are more beautiful.

For the moment, not all grocery stores offer them, but if you have the chance, try them! After all, it's not the appearance that counts, but the taste.

Know the meat and limit your consumption

Purchase less expensive cuts of meat such as lean ground meat, whole chicken, pork shank, and less tender cuts of meat.

Another solution is to reduce your consumption of red meat to lighten your bill. Lentils, tofu, quinoa, and beans are vegetable proteins that cost less and are worth discovering.

Check the expiry dates.

First of all, it must be recognized that an expiry date does not necessarily mean that the food must be discarded as soon as it is "overdue." These dates are often only indicators to remind you when the product can be consumed to its fullest. That is, when the food is to its fullest taste, full texture, or nutritional value. However, care must be taken since the expiry date only applies when the product is not open. From the opening, the date no longer applies.

There is nothing stopping you from picking up the items from the bottom to get food at the grocery store, the date of which is as far away as possible. They will be better longer, and you will avoid food waste.

Look at the bottom and top shelves.

When next you visit the grocery store, notice that the most popular and expensive products are placed at the height of your eyes. Make a habit of looking at the top shelves, where the lesser-known are and often more affordable commodities, and lower shelves, which usually have staple foods.

Fewer than one in two checks the quantity information when making purchases. However, the first thing to do is to compare the price of items of the same nature. Taking two blocks of cheese and choosing the cheapest is not necessarily the best deal. It is necessary to know how to compare the price to the unit of measure, either by 100 g or 100 ml, and not only the selling price. To quickly compare different formats, consult the tablet label; the price per unit of measure is still listed.

Increasingly, consumers are confused at the variety of formats present. They have trouble figuring out which product is the cheapest. Often, this will lead them to choose products on sale. However, these are not necessarily cheaper than those posted at current prices. Even for products you regularly buy, always evaluate the unit price. That's the thing.

Beware of large formats.

What about family, jumbos, and economic formats? At first glance, they seem more profitable. However, it is not always true to think that large formats are more interesting than small ones. To be certain, follow the trick: consult the label of the price per unit, either by 100 g or 100 ml, and compare!

Also, be aware that just getting bigger sizes can push you to increase portions. As a result, your family box could very well empty as quickly as if you had bought the small format. Result: the economy is no longer there!

Minimize individual packages

As they are very practical, we often tend to minimize the amount of individual packaging we buy. Whether it's a small container of yogurt, compote, juice, or a packaged cake, these products generally have a much higher unit price. Of course, these products represent a winning solution for families. With lunches and children, single servings remain very convenient, and we are ready to pay a little more.

On the other hand, if time permits, the solution is to turn to bulk foods or bigger sizes (if, of course, it's better) and makes small individual portions in advance. In this way, you can dose portions yourself, and it will be more convenient when you make the lunches. Consider this tip for your next meal planning!

Alter the different brands in your basket

In the past, private labels were often viewed negatively by consumers. Rumor had it that the products we're selling at a lower price because of poorer quality compared to the private label. Now, people are finding that food is just as delicious and, above all, more affordable. Home brands are much improved and have increased their quality standard.

Adopt frozen fruits and vegetables

A frozen food section is an interesting option for your budget. This section allows you to enjoy good fruits and vegetables throughout the year, and at a reasonable price. However, choose blends in their natural state, without adding salt, fat, or sugar.

Claim a deferred coupon

A product is announced in a circular, and it remains in the display? Do not be shy and ask for your postponement: you are entitled to it. Also, know that it is valid at all times.

In addition, if the item is no longer available, supermarkets must offer something of the same nature and the same price.

Take a look at the time of the transaction.

The last step before you proclaim pro supermarket is always to check the registration of your products at the checkout. Would you not want to break all your efforts into a simple price error? Too often, it is these small blunders that ruin your savings. Please note that according to the price accuracy policy, when there is an error and the item is less than $ 10, the merchant must give you the product free of charge.

In the end, double-check your grocery bill.

Small impulsive fishing: stay tuned!

Good smells

Immediately you walk through at the front door of your supermarket, a good smell of roast chicken tickles your nostrils. Do you know that this smell could make you spend more? According to a study carried out, adding odors in a store increases purchase intentions by 80%.

Why do you feel good fresh bread automatically makes you want to buy some? Odors are directly related to the part of the brain where the emotions sit. The brain analyzes perfumes without our being aware of them, which significantly influences our purchasing behavior.

Of course, few people do not like to smell freshly baked bread. It's more pleasant to do your market when it smells good. Just be aware of the smells that sometimes lead to unplanned purchases.

The music

At the grocery store, a customer stops about three seconds in an alley to make his choice. Do you know that this figure can vary according to the musical rhythm broadcast in supermarkets? Indeed, the more the melody is slow and pleasant, the more you will move slowly and, at the same time, the more you will spend. For example, you will think more about the choices to make; you will analyze the promotional posters, you will take the time to read the labels, etc.

On the other hand, if your grocery store plays fast music, you will be inclined to impulsive purchases. In either case, try to keep the focus on your grocery list. If you wish, bring your own music!

The stickers

The allegations as 100% natural, made with real fruit, light, with added calcium, fat, etc., are all indicators that reassure us as a consumer. However, focusing on one of these criteria is distracting from nutrition information.

A box of cookies that displays without trans-fat, cholesterol, and low saturated fat is still a fat and sweet product. However, the health criteria mentioned in large print make us forget the other's other nutritional characteristics. This is confusing to the consumer who always wants to make the best choices.

The solution is to take the time to read the labels and the list of ingredients. Try not to buy products whose list contains words that are too complicated to pronounce. The important thing is to choose foods that have the fewest ingredients possible.

In addition, compare the products with each other: the original product and the one with 40% less fat, for example. A "light" food does not mean it is healthier because to make it less fat, some manufacturers often compensate with sugar or other harmful ingredients to maintain texture and taste.

The discounts 2 for 1, 3 for 5

Supermarkets sometimes offer types of discounts that encourage consumers to buy beyond their needs. Balances such as three canned soups for $5 are a good example, as they can make you want to automatically take three when in reality, you only need two. Remember that in most grocery stores, prices are set individually. If you buy only one item, you will only pay for that quantity.

Tasting kiosks

Who has never been tempted by a bite to eat at the tasting booth? These small stands are a real cute catch! Of course, you do not have to do without it ... It's still a little grocery. On the other hand, we must know that this sometimes pushes us to make unexpected purchases. Stay alert and ask yourself the question: do I really need this week?

Tastings are a good way to discover new products and vary the menus. If you like the product you like, it will still be possible to get it the following week. As a bonus, they sometimes offer discounts or coupons to use on the next purchase. This is a double reason to wait until later to switch to a planned purchase mode!

Displays

Grocery stores like to create displays of products by association, that is to say, by making special arrangements such as a "special Italy" with Pasta and sauces, chocolate for fondue near berries, or salad vinaigrette near the vegetables. On the one hand, it enhances food while suggesting combinations of ideas to consumers. On the other hand, it may encourage us to go beyond our needs. Often, these products are not necessarily on sale. We must remain vigilant!

Example of 1 Week Mediterranean Diet List

Monday

Breakfast: 1 egg + 1 slice of low-fat white cheese + whole wheat bread + Tomato, cucumber

Lunch: Tuna with lots of green Salad + 1 slice of whole wheat bread

Search: Semi-skimmed milk + Almond

Evening: A vegetable dish with olive oil + half-fat yogurt + Salad

Snack: Fruit

Tuesday

Breakfast: 2 slices of white cheese + Olive + Bran bread + Tomato, cucumber, greens

Noon: Baked, grilled vegetables + Pasta + Ayran

Search: Fruit + nuts

Evening: Legumes dinner with olive oil + half-fat yogurt + Salad

Search: Semi-skimmed milk + Fruit

Wednesday

Breakfast: Half-fat yogurt + 3 spoons of oatmeal + Fruit

Lunch: cheese, avocado salad + whole wheat bread + buttermilk

Search: Semi-skimmed milk + walnut

Evening: Grilled fish + lush Salad

Search: Fruit

Thursday

Breakfast: Cheese omelet + olives + bran bread + Greens

Lunch: Legumes with olive oil + Half-fat yogurt + Salad

Search: Fruit + Almond

Evening: A vegetable meal with olive oil + Bulgur pilaf + Ayran

Search: Half-fat yogurt + walnut

Friday

Breakfast: Curd cheese + Walnut + Bran bread + Tomato, cucumber

Noon: Salad with boiled lentils + buttermilk

Search: 1 bowl of yogurt + Fruit

Evening: Vegetable meal + salad + bran bread with olive oil

Search: Fruit

Saturday

Breakfast: Semi-skimmed milk + Hazelnut + 2 tablespoons of oatmeal + Fruit

Noon: Pasta with vegetables + buttermilk + salad

Search: Fruit + walnut

Evening: Grilled Chicken + Half-fat yogurt + Boiled vegetables

Search: Semi-skimmed milk + Fruit

market

Breakfast: Menemen + Half Fat White Cheese + Bran Bread + Greens

Noon: sandwich + buttermilk made from whole grain bread

Search: Fruit + Almond

Evening: Soup + Legumes meal with olive oil + Salad

Search: Semi-skimmed milk

Mediterranean Recipes

Lettuce Tacos with Chicken to the Shepherd

Preparation time: 1 h 20 minutes

Cooking time: 35 minutes

6 Servings

Ingredients

50 grams of achiote for the marinade

1/4 cup of apple vinegar for the marinade

3 pieces of guajillo chile clean, deveined and seedless, hydrated for the marinade

2 pieces of wide chili clean, deveined and seedless, hydrated for the marinade

3 garlic cloves for the marinade

1/4 piece of white onion for the marinade

1/2 cup pineapple juice for marinade

1 tablespoon salt marinade

1 tablespoon fat pepper for marinade

2 pieces of clove for the marinade

1 tablespoon oregano for the marinade

1 piece of roasted guaje tomato, for the marinade

1 tablespoon cumin for the marinade

1 piece of boneless and skinless chicken breast, cut into small cubes

1 tablespoon of olive or flax oil

Enough of French Lettuce Eva

1/2 piece of pineapple cut into half moons

1/2 cup chopped coriander

1/2 cup finely chopped purple onion

To the taste of tree chili sauce to accompany

To the taste of lemon to accompany

Preparation

1. For the marinade, blend the achiote, vinegar, chilies, garlic, onion, juice, salt, pepper, cloves, oregano, tomato, and cumin until a homogeneous mixture is obtained.
2. Put the chicken and the marinade inside a bowl with the shepherd marinade for 1 hour in refrigeration.
3. Heat a pan over medium heat with the oil and cook the chicken you marinated until it is cooked. Reserve covered.
4. Heat a grill over high heat, roast the pineapple until golden brown, remove and cut into cubes, reserve.
5. On a table place sheets of French Lettuce Eva®, add the chicken to the shepherd and serve with the roasted pineapple, cilantro, onion, served with a little sauce and lemons.

Nutritional information

Percentage of daily values based on a 2,000-calorie diet.

Calories   92.2   kcal 4.6%

Carbohydrates   22.3   g 7.4%

Proteins   1.6   g 3.2%

Lipids   0.9   g 1.3%

Dietary fiber   2.9   g 5.8%

Sugars   6.6   g 7.4%

Cholesterol   0.0   mg 0.0%

Colorful Vegetable Strudel
Cooking time: 30 to 60 min

Servings: 2

Ingredients

For the vegetable strudel:

- 1 pkg of puff pastry
- 1/2 head of broccoli
- 3 carrots
- 1/2 head of caramel
- 1 bell pepper (red)

- 2 garlic cloves
- Caraway (ground)
- salt
- Pepper (from the mill)
- 1 egg (to brush)
- 1 onion For the Béchamel sauce:
- 50 g of butter
- 50 g of flour
- 250 ml of milk For the herb sauce:
- 1 pinch of nutmeg (ground)
- 200 g of yogurt
- 125 g sour cream
- 1/2 bunch chives
- 1/2 bunch of parsley
- some dill (fresh)
- salt
- pepper

Preparation:

1. For the colorful vegetable strudel from the Air fryer first or you use an oven, wash the vegetables, clean and cut into bite-sized pieces. Brew in boiling salted water for about 2 minutes. Drain well.
2. Peel garlic including the onions and cut into small cubes.

3. For the béchamel sauce, melt the butter, adding first the flour and then the milk, stirring constantly. Add garlic, onion, vegetables, salt, pepper and cumin.
4. Roll out the puff pastry and then put the stuffing on the lower third. Beat in the sides and roll up the dough to a firm vortex.
5. Whisk the egg and brush the whirlpool with it.
6. Bake for approximately 25 minutes at 180 ° C in the Air Fryer.

In the meantime, prepare the herb sauce. For chopped chives, parsley and dill finely. Stir all Ingredients until smooth and season the sauce.

Serve vegetable strudel from the hot air fryer with herb sauce. Colorful vegetable strudel from the Air fryer also tastes cold.

Nutritional Information:

Calories 286.6

Total Fat 8.6 g

Saturated Fat 2.5 g

Polyunsaturated Fat 1.5 g

Monounsaturated Fat 2.5 g

Cholesterol 48.2 mg

Sodium 916.3 mg

Potassium 362.4 mg

Total Carbohydrate 37.5 g

Dietary Fiber 6.7 g

Sugars 2.5 g

Protein 15.8 g

Creamy Strawberry cup
For one person

Preparation time: 10 mins

Freezing time: 30 mins

To make this delicious ice cream we need:

<u>Ingredients:</u>

- 500 gr of very ripe raspberries
- 25 cl of cooking cream
- 235 gr of sugar

Preparation:

All you have to do put all the ingredients in the blender, and we are going to beat it little by little until you achieve the desired texture, and then put it in the freezer in a silicone mold, leave it in at least 30 minutes.

Nutritional Information

- 20% Total Fat 13g
- 41% Saturated Fat 8.2g.
- Trans Fat 0g
- 18% Cholesterol 53mg
- 4% Sodium 96mg
- 7% Potassium 262mg
- 10% Total Carbohydrates 30g
- 7% Dietary Fiber 1.8g

Apple Green Ceviche
3 Servings

Preparation time: 10 minutes

Cooking time: 20 minutes

Ingredients

- 1/4 cup of lemon juice
- 1/3 cup of orange juice
- 2 tablespoons of olive oil
- 1/4 bunch of cilantro
- 2 pieces of green apple without peel, cut into medium cubes
- 1 piece of finely chopped serrano chili
- 1 cup of jicama cut into medium cubes
- 1 piece of avocado cut into cubes
- 1 cup cucumber cut into cubes
- 1/4 bunch of finely chopped basil leaf
- 1/4 cup of finely chopped cilantro
- 1 pinch of salt
- 1 piece of sliced radish

- 1 piece of serrano chili cut into slices
- 1/4 piece of purple onion

Preparation

1. Add lemon juice, orange juice, olive oil and cilantro to the blender. Blend perfectly well. Reservation.
2. Add to a bowl the apple, serrano pepper, jicama, avocado, cucumber, basil, cilantro, mix with the preparation of the blender and season perfectly well.
3. Serve the ceviche in a deep dish and decorate with the radish the chile serrano and the purple onion. Enjoy

Nutritional information

- Percentage of daily values based on a 2,000-calorie diet.
- Calories   61.9   kcal 3.1%
- Carbohydrates   14.4   g 4.8%
- Proteins   1.6   g 3.1%
- Lipids   0.3   g 0.4%
- Sugars   6.2   g 6.9%
- Cholesterol   0.0   mg 0.0%

Vegetable and Kale Soup

Preparation time: 10 minutes

Cooking time: 30 minutes

Ingredients

2 Servings

   2 tablespoons of olive oil

   1/2 piece of white onion filleted

   1 celery stick cut in cubes

   1 cup chopped pore

   1 tablespoon finely chopped garlic

   1 cup sliced mushrooms

   1 cup mushroom filleted

   2 cups of kale

   1/2 piece of fennel the bulb, cut into sticks

   6 cups of beef broth

1 pinch of salt

1 pinch of pepper

1/4 cup of almond

Preparation

1. Heat a medium deep pot over medium heat, add the olive oil, onion and celery until they release the aroma, add the pore, garlic and mushrooms with the mushrooms until they start to release the juice, add the kale until I soften with the fennel. Cook for 5 more minutes.
2. Fill with the beef broth and season to your liking. Cook until it boils, covering it to prevent it from evaporating.
3. Serve in a bowl with a little fresh kale at the end and sliced almonds. Enjoy

Nutritional information

Calories 507 kcal 25%

Carbohydrates 65.6 g 22%

Proteins 35.8 g 72%

Lipids 16.3 g 25%

Dietary fiber 11.9 g 24%

Sugars 10.7 g 12%

Cholesterol 0.0 mg 0.0%

Mediterranean salad
Preparation: 10 mins

Freezing Time: 30 mins

Number of Serving: 1

The Mediterranean salad is also famous as a Greek salad, although do not believe it, the Hellenes are the only ones who do not call it this way. This consists of groceries typical of the Mediterranean area, such as green leaves and radishes. The tomato formed a part of this recipe until eighteen hundred and eighteen, the year in which this edible became popular in this territory.

Ingredients

Now, we pass you the precise ingredients so that you can make this salad recipe that you like so much:

- ✓ Two cups peeled cucumber, seeded in squares
- ✓ Two red colored tomatoes, in squares
- ✓ Green bell pepper, in squares
- ✓ Purple onion, thin slices or half moons
- ✓ Cup sliced black olives
- ✓ Cup feta cheese, collapsed
- ✓ Tablespoons olive oil
- ✓ Tablespoons red wine vinegar
- ✓ Dried thyme spoon
- ✓ Dried oregano spoon
- ✓ Sea salt and black pepper, to taste

Preparation

These are the simple steps of the recipe for your Mediterranean food and diet menu:

Mix each and every ingredient in a bowl.

You can eat instantly or let marinate in the refrigerator thirty minutes before eating so that the flavors have time to mix well.

Serve as you can see in the picture, with cheeses, cookies and serrano ham or with your favorite accompaniment.

Nutritional Value:

Protein: 6.9 g

Total Fat: 16.1 g

Calories: 241.6

Saturated Fat: 2.9 g

Grilled Fish with Vegetables

The trick of preparing this dish is not to displace the fish until it has formed a crust and has detached itself from the pan, so use your little kitchen alarm chicken and do not touch it until it sounds.

Preparation: 10 mins

Cooking Time: 5 mins

Number of Serving: 1

Ingredients

The ingredients to make the dish are very simple:

✓ Fish
✓ Vegetables
✓ Salt

Preparation

Recipe steps for your Mediterranean food and diet menu:

To adapt the fish or to acquire it made fillets or supreme, to spread it with a mixture of oil, salt and pepper.

Garnish and slice the vegetables (zucchini, onion, red pepper, etc.) and trim some asparagus. Put everything on an iron or a pan over high heat salpimentando vegetables. Go brushing the fish from time to time with the oil mixture.

Plating the fish and vegetables that each one likes best and eating warm.

Nutritional Value:

Calories   260.7

Total Fat   2.6 g

Saturated Fat   0.4 g

Polyunsaturated Fat   1.3 g

Monounsaturated Fat 0.3 g

Cholesterol   164.9 mg

Sodium   207.0 mg

Potassium   1,577.7 mg

Total Carbohydrate   10.9 g

Dietary Fiber 3.8 g

Sugars 5.5 g

Protein 47.7 g

Garlic Chicken with an Olive Jet
With some frequency, the easiest recipes are the most effective. Garlic chicken attests to this maxim. Unmistakable and full of colors, this dish is part of the great recipe book of the Mediterranean food of Spain.

Preparation: 10 mins

Cooking Time: 20 mins

Number of Serving: 1

Ingredients

 ✓ The ingredients to make the dish are very simple and cheap:

- ✓ 1 kg free range chicken
- ✓ Ten cloves of garlic
- ✓ One hundred fifty ml white wine
- ✓ Lauro leaf
- ✓ Parsley to taste

Preparation

It is the moment to decide if we want to cook the chicken with skin or without it. The 2 options are valid. Once we have decided, we will season the chicken chopped on each and every side and reserve it.

We take a pan, we squirt olive oil, and we peeled garlic cloves. When the oil is hot we lower it to medium power and let the garlic fall. Once golden brown we take it out so that it has just been made out of the pan.

Holding the medium intensity, we throw the chicken until it is browned by each and every one of the parts.

When we have it, we reserve it and store the oil used. Without moving that medium power, we add the garlic cloves, the lauro, and the wine and remove each and every one of the ingredients. We leave it for twenty minutes at low power.

Once the wine has evaporated, we take it out and serve it in a fountain. We already have it.

Nutritional Value:

184 Cal

0% Carbs

41% 8g Fat

59% 26g Protein

Grilled Hake and Vegetables Recipe

This recipe for fresh hake fillets and grilled vegetables is a good combination and a good option for a healthy meal.

Preparation: 10 mins

Cooking Time: 15 mins

Number of Serving: 2

Ingredients for four people:

- ✓ 4 fresh hake fillets
- ✓ 1 bunch fresh asparagus
- ✓ 5 tomatoes
- ✓ 300 g mushrooms
- ✓ 200 g of standard peppers
- ✓ 4 crushed garlic cloves
- ✓ 40 ml of extra virgin olive oil Arbequina
- ✓ Salt to taste
- ✓ 1 lemon

How to make the recipe for grilled hake and vegetables

Start the oven at 150 ° C

Split the lemon in two and with a half sprinkle the hake. Reserve

Clean tomatoes, asparagus, mushrooms and standard peppers with water, dry with paper towels.

Slice the mushrooms and sprinkle with the other half of the lemon, set aside.

Cut the tomatoes into slices a centimeter thick, set aside.

Cut the hard part of the asparagus, reserve.

Put the roasting pan on the fire, when it has been heated, sprinkle with olive oil and put the asparagus, leave a few minutes, turn around, leave a few more minutes, take out and put on a suitable baking sheet.

On the same plate, roast the mushrooms a few minutes on each side, remove and put on the tray with the asparagus.

In the same plate place the tomato slices, spread over half the crushed garlic and salt to taste, let it roast for a few minutes and turn it over, let it do a few more minutes, remove and place on the tray with asparagus and mushrooms. Insert the tray into the oven to keep it warm,

On the same plate (put a little more oil if necessary) Roast the fresh hake fillets, add salt to taste, leave about five minutes on each side, remove and leave on another tray or plate inside the oven.

In a skillet sprinkled with oil, brown the other half of crushed garlic and heat it over the hake fillets.

In the same pan that the garlic has browned, add the standard peppers, add salt on top and leave a few minutes turning them occasionally. Remove and place in the vegetable tray.

Serve right away.

Nutritional Value:

Calories 92

Fat 1.77g

Carbs 0.17g

Protein 17.79g

Asparagus Pudding and Gluten-Free Cheese Pudding Recipe

This asparagus and cheese pudding-suffle is gluten-free because the breadcrumbs it carries are gluten-free, but it can be made with normal bread if you have no problem with gluten.

Preparation: 10 mins

Cooking Time: 25 mins

Number of Serving: 2

Ingredients for a 20 × 20 mold:

- ✓ 1 bunch of asparagus
- ✓ 1 large onion
- ✓ 1 handful of cherry tomatoes
- ✓ 100 g breadcrumbs without grated gluten
- ✓ 150 g grated gruyere cheese
- ✓ 150 ml of semi eco warm milk (can be almond or oat milk)
- ✓ 90 g of melted eco butter

- ✓ 2 fresh free range eggs with separated yolks
- ✓ Salt and pepper to taste
- ✓ 1 tablespoon extra-virgin olive oil

How to prepare asparagus and cheese pudding

Start the oven at 185 ºC

Spread a mold of a liter of capacity with butter, set aside.

Clean the asparagus with cold water and cut them into pieces. Peel off the onion and then slice it into thin slices.

Put the oil in a pan, heat and poach the onion, when it is already transparent, add the asparagus and leave a few minutes, turn off the heat and set aside.

Pour the breadcrumbs into a large bowl, add the grated cheese, warm milk, egg yolks, mix well until everything is integrated. Salt and pepper

Raise the egg white to the point of snow and pour it into the bowl, mix carefully from the bottom up, until everything is well mixed.

Pour all the prepared in the mold and take to the oven about thirty-forty minutes or until we see it golden brown.

Nutritional Value:

Calories: 155 calories

Fat: 10.8 g

Carbohydrates: 3.3 g

Fiber: 2.3 g

Protein: 9 g

Timbale Of Scalded

You can make it simple or bake it with some bechamel. Either option is absolutely delicious. Try it! You will repeat.

Servings: 4 people

Time: 1 hour and 50 minutes

Ingredients

- ✓ 4 potatoes
- ✓ 2 eggplants
- ✓ 2 red peppers
- ✓ 150 g curling goat cheese
- ✓ Salt pepper

For the sofrito:

- ✓ 2 tomatoes
- ✓ 2 onions
- ✓ ½ green pepper
- ✓ 1 clove garlic
- ✓ Olive oil

Preparation

Wash the potatoes and then cook them in salt water 40 min. Peel and cut into slices. Cut the cheese into 4 slices. Wash the peppers and eggplants and roast them 50 min at 200 ° C. Remove the pepper and cook the eggplant 20 min more. Peel them, cut them and sprinkle them.

The sofrito: peel and chop the tomato, onion and garlic. Clean and chop the pepper. Stir in oil until soft and season. Arrange in 4 rings a layer of potatoes, one of pepper and another of eggplant. Cover with the sofrito, add the cheese and bake at 180 ° C 15min.

Trick

Ride the scalded like lasagna. Sandwich the pasta sheets, cover with béchamel and bake.

Nutritional Value:

Calories: 260 kcal

`Parmesan Tulips With Salad

you won't leave a leaf or a piece ... of the plate! And we change the crockery for a parmesan tulip. Delicious recipe, delicious presentation.

Servings: 4 people

Preparation and cooking Time: 50 minutes

Ingredients

- ✓ 200 g parmesan
- ✓ 8 cherry tomatoes
- ✓ Salad sprouts
- ✓ 8 quail eggs
- ✓ 4 tablespoons black olives
- ✓ 1 onion
- ✓ 20 g capers
- ✓ 1 can of tuna in oil
- ✓ Oil vinager
- ✓ Lemon juice
- ✓ Mustard, salt, pepper

Preparation

Preheat oven to 160 ° C. Grate the cheese and form with it 4 discs of 15 cm on a baking dish lined with sulfurized paper. Bake for 12 min. Dispose them and put them on bowls so that they take the shape of a tulip and let them cool. Cook the eggs in 5 min salt water, peel them and cut them in half.

Wash the tomatoes and slice them into wedges. Peel the onion and cut it into slices. Wash the shoots. Beat 1 tablespoon of vinegar with 1 mustard, 1 juice, 5 oil, salt and pepper. Distribute all the ingredients with capers, tuna and olives in the tulips. Dress with the vinaigrette and serve immediately.

Trick

To vary the salad, mix some sprouts with currants, apple cubes and some pine nuts. Dress them with oil, Modena vinegar and salt.

Nutritional Value:

Calories: 290 kcal

Salad with fried goat cheese

Preparation time: 5 mins

Cooking Time: 30 minutes

For 4 persons

Homemade crispy rounds of goat cheese on a bed of fresh salad with bell pepper

Ingredients

- ✓ 100 gr mixed salad
- ✓ One red pepper
- ✓ 200 gr fresh goat cheese (rounds)
- ✓ One large egg
- ✓ Oil for frying
- ✓ One tablespoon finely chopped almond
- ✓ One plate of breadcrumbs
- ✓ One plate of flour

- ✓ Dressing
- ✓ Pepper and salt
- ✓ One tablespoon honey
- ✓ Two teaspoons lemon
- ✓ olive juice
- ✓ Three tablespoons oil

Preparation

1. Make sure that the goat cheese is well cold; this is the easiest way to work with it. Separate the goat cheese circles (about 12 pieces). Beat the egg on a plate. Mix the goat cheese slices one by one through the flour, then the egg and then the breadcrumbs. And repeat the last two steps (egg and breadcrumbs) for an extra thick and crispy crust.

2. Heat the oil at 180 degrees and fry the balls for 1 minute until they are golden brown. Then drain them on kitchen paper. Separate the seeds from the bell pepper and cut into pieces and fry for 3 minutes with the olive oil in a pan.

3.   Remove the pepper from the pan and pour the baking liquid into a small bowl and combine the lemon juice and honey and season with salt and pepper. Mix this dressing with the salad and add the bell pepper and serve on a plate together with the fried goat cheese. Garnish with some almond.

Nutritional information

Calories   358.2

Total Fat   20.7 g

Saturated Fat   7.9 g

Monounsaturated Fat 7.9 g

Cholesterol   35.9 mg

Potassium   470.6 mg

Total Carbohydrate   33.5 g

Dietary Fiber   4.7 g

Sugars 21.1 g

Protein 14.6 g

Asparagus vegetables from the Air fryer
Cooking time: 15 to 30 min

Ingredients

Servings: 2

4 bars of asparagus (white)

4 bars of asparagus (green)

1 tbsp. butter

One pinch of salt

Pepper

Sugar

Two pcs. Paradeiser (gutted, diced)

100 ml of soup

Two sprigs of lemon balm (leaves peeled, chopped)

Preparation

- For the asparagus Wash the asparagus, peel, remove ends, cut into small pieces and mix with the butter, one pinch of salt, pepper, and sugar.

- Core the Paradeiser and cut into fine cubes.

- Add the asparagus to the baking tray add the soup and heat at 160 ° C in the Philips Air fryer Hot Air Fryer.

- After about 12-15 minutes add the dice and cook for another 5 minutes.

- Then remove the asparagus and stir chopped lemon balm under the finished asparagus.

Nutritional Information

- Total Fat 0.1 g   0%

- Saturated fat 0 g   0%

- Polyunsaturated fat 0.1 g

- Monounsaturated fat 0 g

- Cholesterol 0 mg   0%

- Sodium 2 mg   0%

- Potassium 202 mg   5%

- Total Carbohydrate 3.9 g   1%

- Dietary fiber 2.1 g   8%

- Sugar 1.9 g

- Protein 2.2 g   4%

Beef Roulades

Cooking time: More than 60 min

Ingredients

Servings: 4

- ✓ Four beef schnitzel
- ✓ Salt
- ✓ Pepper
- ✓ Mustard
- ✓ Tomato paste
- ✓ Four slices of bacon (lean)
- ✓ One onion (cut into rings)
- ✓ Pickle
- ✓ 1 cup of rice (cooked)

For the sauce:

- ✓ Roots
- ✓ One onion (medium)
- ✓ 1 Stamper apricot brandy

Preparation

• For the beef roulades, beat the schnitzel, salt, pepper, and coat on one side with tomato paste and mustard. Place the bacon slices on top and spread onion rings, cucumber strips and rice.

- Roll up the schnitzel, fix with a toothpick and fry in Air fryer.

- Take out the beef roulades. Roast the chopped onion and the noodled root system thoroughly in the roasting stock, pour water over it and gently soften the roulades.

- Before serving, pass the vegetables with the juice to a sauce. Cook well and deglaze with apricot brandy. Just season if necessary.

- Pour the sauce over the beef roulades and serve them hot.

To beef roulades also match potatoes.

Nutritional Information

Saturated Fat 6.4g grams

Trans Fat 0.7g grams

Polyunsaturated Fat 1g grams

Monounsaturated Fat 8.3g grams

41%Cholesterol 123mg milligrams

35%Sodium 844mg milligrams

15%Potassium 538mg milligrams

5%Total Carbohydrates 14g grams

5% Dietary Fiber 1.2g grams

Sugars 6.1g grams

Protein 27g

Grilled chicken with ranch sauce
Preparation: 30 min

Baking: 1 h 25 min

Maceration: 12 h

Servings: 4

Ingredients

- Chicken
- 1 lb. chicken (4 lb.)
- 10 ml (2 teaspoons) salt
- 5 ml (1 teaspoon) of garlic powder
- ½ lemons
- 1 recipe of ranch vinaigrette
- Salad
- 4 celery stalks, minced
- 1 bulb of fennel, finely chopped
- 1 green onion, chopped
- 30 ml (2 tablespoons) chopped fennel leaves
- 30 ml (2 tablespoons) of olive oil
- 15 ml (1 tablespoon) lemon juice

Preparation

Chicken

1. On a work surface, using the chef's knife or kitchen scissors, remove the bone from the back of the chicken. Flip the chicken and cut in half in the center of the breasts. Place the pieces in a large glass dish. Sprinkle chicken skin with salt and garlic powder. Rub the outside and rthen inside of the chicken with the cut part of the lemon. Thoroughly coat with 1/2 cup (125 mL) ranch vinaigrette. Cover and refrigerate 12 hours.

2. Preheat half barbecue at high power. Oil the grill on the off side.

3. Drain the meat. Place the chicken on the off-the-grill section, skin side on the grill. Close the barbecue lid. Bake 45 minutes while maintaining a temperature of 200 ° C (400 ° F). Return the chicken and continue cooking for 35 minutes or until a thermometer inserted in the thigh, without touching the bone, indicates 180 ° F (82 ° C) maintaining a

temperature of 200 ° C (400 ° F).
Finish cooking on the lit section of
the barbecue to mark the chicken.

Salad

4. Meanwhile, in a bowl, mix all
   ingredients. Salt and pepper.
5. Cut the chicken into pieces. Serve
   with the salad and the rest of the
   ranch vinaigrette.

Nutritional Value:

Sodium: 748.6 mg

Total Carbohydrate: 9.1 g

Calories: 178.5

Protein: 28.3 g

Scallops with Spinach

Meat and vegetables, the perfect combination. This second dish will be ideal in a light and healthy menu and even for a celebration. Look at the recipe and succeed.

Servings: 4 people

Time: 20 minutes

Ingredients

- ✓ 8 thin beef steaks
- ✓ 8 slices of ham
- ✓ 3 tablespoons butter
- ✓ 8 sage leaves
- ✓ 1 glass of white wine
- ✓ Salt pepper

For the garnish:

- ✓ 5 potatoes
- ✓ 1 clove garlic
- ✓ 75 g butter
- ✓ 300 g spinach
- ✓ Olive oil and salt

Preparation

Wash your potatoes and cook them in salt water 35 min. Peel and mix with butter, salt and pepper. Pass them through the pass-through. Clean and chop the spinach. Cook them in salted water, 5 min. Sauté the chopped garlic in oil, add the spinach and redo them 1 min. Season the steaks, spread the ham and roll them.

Tie the rolls with kitchen thread, with a sage leaf. Donate them 4 min in a pan with 2 tablespoons of butter. Remove them Pour the wine into the pan, bring to a boil and scrape the bottom. Season, add the rest of the butter and stir. Add the rolls, wrap and serve with the vegetables and mash.

Trick

The sauce will be tastier if, while adding the white wine, add a little lemon zest and 2 tablespoons of juice.

Nutritional Value:

Calories: 565 kcal

Total Carbohydrate   6.1 g

Dietary Fiber 1.7 g

Sugars 2.1 g

Protein 15.1 g

Beef Dish WITH Bird Lettuce
Cooking time: More than 60 min

Servings: 4

Ingredients

- 600 g boiled beef (cooked)
- 6 cl of Sherry Dry
- 2 carrots
- 2 turnips (yellow)
- 1/4 celeriac
- 4 tablespoons of chives (chopped)
- 600 ml of beef soup
- 10 sheets of gelatin
- Vegetable oil (for the form)
- Pepper (from the mill)
- Salt
- 200 g of bird's lettuce

- Pumpkinseed-pesto
- Chives (to sprinkle)

For The Marinade:

- 4 tablespoons of corn oil
- 3 tablespoons apple cider vinegar
- 2 tablespoons of beef soup
- Pinch of salt

Preparation

1. Boil the soup with 200 ml of water.
2. Add carrots, yellow turnips and celery and cook until soft. Remove from the soup, let cool and cut into 3 mm thick strips.
3. Soak the gelatin inside cold water, squeeze and add to the soup. Season well with sherry, salt and pepper and remove from Air fryer heat.
4. Spread the terrine mold with little oil, insert the plastic wrap lengthwise and smooth with kitchen paper.
5. Cut the top of the heated beef from the Air fryer (preferably with the bread slicer) into 2 mm thick slices, dip each slice into the still warm

soup one at a time and line the shape with it. In doing so, arrange overlapping about 6 cm over the edge.

6. Pour in a little soup, sprinkle with chives, place the vegetable strips lengthways and top them dipped in soup. Repeat this process three times; Pour in the rest of the soup.

7. Press foil and refrigerate for 3 hours. For the marinade, mix all ingredients with a whisk and marinate the lettuce. Toss the terrine, remove the foil and cut into slices.

8. Arrange on chilled plates and garnish with the marinated lettuce. Drizzle with pumpkin seed pesto and sprinkle with chives.

Tip

Depending on the season, the vegetable inlay of the Sulz can be modified with radishes, asparagus or pickled mushrooms. Drizzled with apple cider vinegar and sprinkled with Fleur de sel and pepper, the Sulz tastes even spicier.

Nutrition Information

- 221kcal
- Fat: 13g
- Saturated fat: 7g
- Carbohydrates: 1g
- Protein: 23g

Quinoa Salad

Preparation: 5 mins

Cooking Time: 10 mins

Number of Serving:

Ingredients

- ✓ 100 g of varied green leaf
- ✓ 100 g black quinoa
- ✓ 1 large fennel
- ✓ 80 g rolled almond
- ✓ 2 tbsp of nutritional yeast
- ✓ 2 tbsp hemp seeds
- ✓ Apple vinager
- ✓ extra virgin olive oil
- ✓ Salt

Preparation

After cooking and draining the quinoa, wash and dry the lettuce well. Place the almonds in a pan and simmer them over low heat so they don't burn. Mix the lettuce with quinoa and fennel carpaccio. Sprinkle the almonds, dress with a pinch of salt, yeast, seeds, a dash of vinegar and oil. Remove and serve.

Nutritional Value:

Calories: 383;

Total Fat: 19g;

Saturated Fat: 4g;

Cholesterol: 12mg;

Carbohydrate: 43g;

Protein: 12g

Salad with Feta Cheese

Preparation: 5 mins

Number of Serving: 1 person

Ingredients

- ✓ 100 g of varied green leaf
- ✓ 2 tomatoes
- ✓ 100 g feta cheese
- ✓ 1 avocado
- ✓ 100 g quinoa
- ✓ Extra virgin olive oil
- ✓ Salt

Preparation

When you have finished preparing the quinoa, wash and dry the lettuce well. Cut the tomatoes, feta cheese and avocados. Mix the ingredients with the lettuce and quinoa. Dress with a pinch of salt and oil. Remove and serve.

Nutritional Value:

Protein: 4.6 g

Total Fat: 3.1 g

Calories: 91.8

Saturated Fat: 2.1 g

Quinoa Carrot Cake
Preparation: 20 mins

Cooking Time: 50 mins

Number of Serving: 2 persons

Ingredients

- ✓ 500 g of carrots
- ✓ 200 g quinoa
- ✓ 4 eggs
- ✓ 80 g of cane sugar
- ✓ 1 teaspoon chopped ginger
- ✓ Lemon zest
- ✓ 200 g of white cheese spread
- ✓ 1 skimmed yogurt
- ✓ 100 g icing brown sugar
- ✓ 1 teaspoon of sugar

- ✓ 1 carrot to decorate
- ✓ Sunflower oil for the mold
- ✓ Sea salt

Preparation

To start, cook and let the quinoa cool. Peel and chop the carrots. Cook them in a saucepan with water for 20 minutes, drain them and pass them through a passage. Preheat the oven to 180 ° C. Next, separate the whites from the yolks. Beat the yolks first alone and then with the sugar until they double in volume.

Add the chopped ginger, lemon zest, quinoa and carrot puree. Stir slowly until the ingredients are integrated. Mount the egg whites with little salt and incorporate the dough with slow movements to try to lower them as little as possible.

Divide the dough into two round molds greased with sunflower oil and a pinch of sprinkled flour. Bake for 25 or 30 minutes. Remove the dough from the oven and let it cool. Prepare the topping by mixing the cheese with the yogurt. Add the sugar little by little.

Beat slowly until everything is well integrated. Place a cake on a plate or pan. Cover with the cream cheese and place the second cake on top. Cover the top and sides with the rest of the cream cheese. Decorate the top with grated carrot.

Nutritional Value:

Amount Per serving (1 slice)

Calories 290Calories from Fat 171

% Daily Value*

Fat 19g29%

Saturated Fat 7g44%

Cholesterol 35mg12%

Sodium 23mg1%

Potassium 155mg4%

Carbohydrates 25g8%

Fiber 3g13%

Sugar 14g16%

Protein 6g12%

Squids Stuffed With Quinoa And Vegetables

Preparation: Approx. 10 mins

Cooking Time: 30 mins

Number of Serving: 1 person

Ingredients

- ✓ 8 medium squids
- ✓ 250 g quinoa
- ✓ 1 onion
- ✓ 1 carrot
- ✓ 3 tomatoes
- ✓ 2 bay leaves
- ✓ Pepper
- ✓ Salt
- ✓ olive oil
- ✓ Dried oregano

Preparation

Peel the tomatoes, chop them and sauté them for 10 minutes in a pan with two tablespoons of oil, the washed bay leaf and a little oregano. Pepper and reserve. Then clean the squid and wash them (leave the whole bodies and chop the legs and fins). Scrape and wash the carrot, and peel the onion. Chop them and redo them 5 minutes in 1 tablespoon of oil. Add the legs and fins, and cook a few more minutes. Add the washed quinoa, cover with a glass of water, season and cook for 8 or 10 minutes until the quinoa has absorbed the liquid. Fill the squid with the previous mixture and close them with chopsticks. Cook them in tomato sauce, covered and simmered, about 10 minutes, and serve.

Nutritional Value:

Calories: 340.7

Protein: 16.8 g

Dietary Fiber: 15.5 g

Sodium: 86.0 mg

Sauteed Quinoa and Vegetables

Preparation: 5 mins

Cooking Time: Approx. 20 mins

Number of Serving: 2

Ingredients

- ✓ 300 g quinoa
- ✓ ½ teaspoon of turmeric
- ✓ 1 leek
- ✓ 1 broccoli
- ✓ 2 carrots
- ✓ 50 g of corn
- ✓ 8 tablespoons soy sauce
- ✓ 4 tablespoons apple juice
- ✓ 10 g toasted sesame seeds
- ✓ a few stalks of chives
- ✓ 5 tablespoons olive oil
- ✓ Salt

Preparation

Wash the quinoa and cook it in plenty of water along with the turmeric for 12 or 14 minutes over medium heat. Clean the leek and scrape the carrots, wash them and cut them into strips. Separate the broccoli in twigs, wash them and hide them with the carrot, two minutes. Dip them in cold water and drain them. Rinse and drain the corn.

Heat the oil in a large skillet or wok and sauté the vegetables with the washed and chopped chives and sesame 2 minutes. Add soy and apple juice and stir. Add the quinoa, mix well and serve.

Nutritional Value:

Calories: 340.7

Protein: 16.8 g

Dietary Fiber: 15.5 g

Sodium: 86.0 mg

Pumpkins with Quinoa
Preparation: 5 mins

Cooking Time: Approx. 20 mins

Number of Serving: 2

Ingredients

- ✓ 2 medium violin pumpkins
- ✓ 150 g of tricolor quinoa
- ✓ 200 g cooked chickpeas
- ✓ 30 g of pine nuts
- ✓ 40 g of blueberries
- ✓ Dried reds
- ✓ A few sprigs of parsley
- ✓ 4 tablespoons extra virgin olive oil
- ✓ Salt
- ✓ Pepper
- ✓ 1 teaspoon turmeric
- ✓ 100 g fresh spinach

Preparation

Cut the pumpkins in half lengthwise and, with the help of a spoon, remove the seeds. Place them in a baking dish lined with sulfurized paper and cook in the preheated oven at 200 degrees for 1 hour. Click with a knife to check that they are well cooked, remove from the oven and let it temper.

Wash the quinoa. In a saucepan, boil plenty of salt water and add the quinoa. Cook 20 minutes, drain and reserve. With the assistance of a spoon, empty the pumpkins, leaving a little pulp so as not to break the peel.

Heat a pan with olive oil, add the chopped pumpkin pulp, quinoa, cooked and drained chickpeas, pine nuts, cranberries, and chopped parsley. Season with salt, pepper and a little turmeric. Sauté a couple of minutes and, finally, add fresh spinach. Saute one more minute and remove from heat. Fill the pumpkins with the mixture, sprinkle with a pinch of turmeric and serve.

Nutritional Value:

Calories: 190.

Sugar: 6.4g.

Fat: 6g.

Carbohydrates: 27.3g.

Fiber: 6.8g.

Protein: 7g.

Filet Mignon with Bernese Sauce
Preparation and cooking time: 45 min

4 Servings

Bernese sauce perfectly highlights the flavor of the filet mignon. It is a very rich, elegant and sophisticated dish that you can prepare for a special occasion. Cook the meat with the term you like the most so that each bite is an unforgettable experience.

Ingredients

- ❖ 1/3 cup white vinegar
- ❖ 1/3 cup dry white wine
- ❖ 1 teaspoon of pepper
- ❖ 1 teaspoon minced shallot
- ❖ 2 teaspoons chopped parsley
- ❖ 1/4 of teaspoon of tarragon
- ❖ 3 pieces of egg yolk
- ❖ 4 pieces of beef fillet 2 cm thick

❖ 1 pinch of salt

Preparation

1. Combine wine, vinegar, pepper, shallots and tarragon, heat and reduce to have 1/3 cup. Strain it and reserve.
2. Put a bowl on a water bath, the yolks and the vinegar mixture and heat moving with a balloon whisk to begin to thicken, then put the parsley and remove from heat immediately and set aside.
3. Heat the grill and when it is very hot put a little oil and seal the fillets on the 2 sides, to brown a little and put salt and pepper.
4. Once the steaks are well cooked. Serve immediately with the Bernese sauce.

Nutritional Value:

Total Carbohydrate 4g

1%Dietary Fiber 0.3g

Sugars 1g

Protein 2g

3%Calcium 40mg

7%Iron 1.3mg

Chicken soup with ginger
Yield: 4 servings

Preparation and cooking time: 50 mins

Ingredients

- ❖ Two cooked chicken steaks and chopped
- ❖ Four tablespoons of cooked and chopped carrots
- ❖ 3 cups chicken water
- ❖ A tablespoon of oil
- ❖ A small piece of ginger (not much bigger than a hazelnut), unless you love the spicy taste of this root
- ❖ A grated onion

- ❖ A garlic kernel, chopped
- ❖ One tablespoon of cornstarch
- ❖ Small salt

The preparations

First, onions and garlic must be fried in the oil. Incidentally, the carrot should be cooked with two cups of chicken broth in the blender. Next, this cream should be added onions and garlic porridge. At that time, the ginger had added the recipe, and everything had to cook for a few minutes.

Meanwhile, the cornstarch in the second broth must be dissolved from the rest of the chicken shell. Currently it is continuously cooked and stirred until it thickens. At the last moment, the chicken is incorporated, the salt tasted and served immediately.

Nutritional Value:

Calories per serving: about 150 calories

Chicken with cream and mushrooms
ABOUT 35 MINUTES

Ingredients (1 pers.)

- ❖ Rice
- ❖ 1 chicken leg
- ❖ 1/2 onion
- ❖ Garlic
- ❖ 1 jar of thick cream
- ❖ 1 box of mushrooms
- ❖ Parsley (optional)

Preparation

1. Cook the rice
2. Cut the chicken leg into cubes (or small pieces), onion and mushrooms
3. Fry the garlic and onion in a pan, then add the chicken and mushrooms
4. Simmer
5. Add the cream and rice in the pan
6. Mix
7. It's ready! Enjoy your meal!

Nutritional Value:

Protein: 43.0 g

Total Fat: 8.9 g

Calories: 338.6

Saturated Fat: 2.3 g

Crispy Chicken Thighs with Bacon

Ingredient

- ✓ Four chicken drumsticks (s)
- ✓ Eight slices/ s Bacon, about 100 g
- ✓ Herbs, Mediterranean (rosemary, thyme, oregano, lavender)
- ✓ sea salt
- ✓ 1 tbsp. olive oil

Cooking time: approx. 50 min

Calorie: about 300 kcal

Preparation

1. Preheat oven at 180 ° C (160 ° C convection). Wash the chicken thighs and pat dry.
2. Heat off the olive oil inside a frying pan (if oven suitable) and fry the legs from all sides. Remove from the pan, season well all around (freshly chopped Mediterranean herbs or a high-quality dry mix) and salt. Then wrap with two slices of bacon, if necessary fix with wooden toothpicks, roast again in the still hot pan from above and below. Be careful when turning.
3. Put the pan inside the oven for 30 minutes and add a touch of olive oil if necessary. If there is no pan suitable for cooking, place the legs on the oven rack and push a sheet of baking paper under it as a safety catch, after half the time turn the thighs. Serve hot!

It fits a light raw food salad.

Tip:

Do not use a casserole dish (used in the photo only for decorative purposes). In this, the thighs swim too much in their juice and are therefore not crispy.

Nutritional Information per Piece
- 300 kcal
- 16 g fat (of which 6 g total fat)
- KH 600 mg
- Protein 40 g

Meatball Skewer Recipe

for 4 people

Preparation time: 35 minutes

Cooking time: 25 minutes

Ingredients

500 grams of ground beef

2 cloves of garlic

1 nectarine

1 teaspoon of cumin

1 teaspoon black pepper

1 teaspoon of chili peppers

1 teaspoon of salt

1/2 tea cup of milk

1/2 tea cup of water

1 teaspoon of carbonate

1/2 bunch of dill

1/2 bunch of parsley

2 slices of bread

1 egg

2 red onions (meatballs will be placed between the bottles when stacking.)

Meatball Shish Recipe

You can use oily ground beef for baking.

Meatballs Shish Recipe Cooking Suggestion

Thick chopping the onions will prevent them from being lost during cooking.

Preparation

1. Put the ground beef inside a large bowl, add the bread to the ground beef and knead well.
2. Chop the onions into cubes. Squeeze the juice and add to the ground beef.
3. Crush the garlic in the mortar and add to the mixture, blend with the remaining ingredients.
4. Stretch film and let rest in the cabinet for 30 minutes.
5. After resting, prepare balls the size of apricots.
6. Chop the red onions so that the ring is not too thin.
7. Arrange the patties with the meatballs and onions. Place on a baking sheet with greasy paper.

8. Bake in a pre-heated 180 degree oven for about 25 minutes.
9. Service Suggestion for Meatball Shish Recipe
10. If you wish, you can serve potatoes or rice with apple slices.

Nutritional Information per Piece
- 300 kcal
- 16 g fat (of which 6 g total fat)
- KH 600 mg
- Protein 40 g

Chocolate Mousse
To make this delicate dessert, you need:

<u>Ingredients:</u>

- 250 gr of dark chocolate
- 20 cl of water (you can also put orange juice)
- 1/2 teaspoon ground cinnamon (coffee spoon)
- 2 or 3 crushed hazelnuts to garnish
- 15 ice

Preparation:

1. In a saucepan over medium heat, undo the chocolate with the crushed almonds.
2. We pour the water, and when the mixture is homogeneous, we take it out and cool it in a water bath made with ice.
3. Then we have to beat very well with the rods until it takes a frothy texture.

Nutritional Information

- Calories 225   % Daily Value
- Total Fat 16 g   24%
- Saturated fat 9 g   45%
- Polyunsaturated fat 0.9 g
- Monounsaturated fat 5 g
- Cholesterol 140 mg   46%
- Sodium 38 mg   1%
- Potassium 143 mg   4%
- Total Carbohydrate 16 g   5%
- Dietary fiber 0.6 g   2%
- Sugar 15 g
- Protein 4.1 g   8%

- Caffeine 7 mg
- Vitamin A   10%
- Vitamin C   0%
- Calcium   9%
- Iron   3%
- Vitamin B-6   5%
- Cobalamin   8%
- Magnesium   5%

Vanilla ice cream

Preparation: 15 min

Baking: 15 min

Refrigeration: 3 hours

Freezing: 3 hours

Yield: 625 ML (2 1/2 CUPS)

Ingredients

- 4 egg yolks
- 1/2 cup (125 mL) sugar
- 250 ml (1 cup) of milk, warm
- 250 ml (1 cup) 35% cream, hot

- 1 vanilla pod, split in half lengthwise

Preparation

1. In a pothole or the upper part of a bain-marie, off the heat, whisk the egg yolks and sugar until the mixture is white. Whisk milk, cream, pod and vanilla beans from the pod with the tip of a knife.
2. Cook in a bain-marie stirring with a wooden spoon for about 15 minutes or until the mixture cools the back of the spoon. Remove the vanilla pod, cover and let cool the custard in the refrigerator.
3. If working with an ice cream maker, stir the mixture according to the manufacturer's instructions — freeze (about 45 minutes).
4. If you do not have an ice cream maker, pour the mixture into a large shallow dish and freeze for 2 hours. Stir and freeze again for 1 hour. Transfer the ice cream to the robot and return to the freezer until ready to serve.

Nutritional Information

- 249 calories
- 10g fat (5.7g saturated)
- 7g protein
- 35g carbohydrates (30g sugars or 7.5 tsp.)
- 12mg cholesterol and 43mg sodium

Lemon Strawberry Ice Cream

For 4 people

Ingredients: Whole Liquid Cream (20cl)

Sugar (100g)

Strawberries (500g)

Lemon Juice (3 tablespoons)

Preparation:

1. Place it inside the ice cream maker 24 hours in advance in the freezer.

2. Wash, cut strawberries and mix them.
3. Mix with lemon juice and sugar.
4. Filter the grout to remove solid residues.
5. Add whipped cream to the ice cream maker's bowl.
6. Mix gently.
7. Let turbinate 20 to 30 minutes, and it's ready!

Nutritional Information

- Total Carbohydrate 16 g   5%
- Dietary fiber 0.6 g   2%
- Sugar 15 g
- Protein 4.1 g   8%
- Caffeine 7 mg
- Vitamin A   10%
- Vitamin C   0%
- Calcium   9%
- Iron   3%
- Vitamin B-6   5%
- Cobalamin   8%
- Magnesium   5%

Light Coffee Ice Cream

For 4 people

Ingredients: Skimmed Milk (25cl)

- Light Liquid Cream (8cl)
- Skimmed Milk Powder (15g)
- Coffee in Freeze Dried Powder (100g)
- Egg Yolks (2)
- Sweetener (50g)

Preparation:

1. Put your ice cream maker vat 24 hours in advance in the freezer.
2. Mix the milk, milk powder and half of the sweetener in a saucepan over low heat.
3. Beat the yolks with the remaining sweetener until the mixture whitens.
4. Add the coffee, then the hot milk while mixing.
5. Let cool an hour, then an hour in the refrigerator.

6. Add the whipped cream with a mixer in the bowl of your ice cream maker.
7. Mix everything gently.
8. Let turbinate 20 to 30 minutes, and its ready!

Nutritional Information

- Total Carbohydrate 16 g   5%
- Dietary fiber 0.6 g   2%
- Sugar 15 g
- Protein 4.1 g   8%
- Caffeine 7 mg
- Vitamin A   10%
- Vitamin C   0%
- Calcium   9%
- Iron   3%
- Vitamin B-6   5%
- Cobalamin   8%
- Magnesium   5%

Nutella Ice Cream

For 4 people

Ingredients: Nutella (220g)

- Egg Yolks (4)
- Whole Liquid Cream (20cl)
- Sugar (20g)
- Water (20cl)
- Salt (1 pinch)

Preparation:

1. Place it inside the ice cream maker 24 hours in advance in the freezer.
2. Separate the whites from the yellows by keeping only 2 whites out of 4.
3. Make syrup with the sugar and water by heating the mixture over high heat for 30 seconds.
4. Let cool a little and mix the syrup with the yolks with a mixer.
5. Mount the two whites in the snow with a pinch of salt.
6. Add whipped cream to the ice cream maker's bowl.

7. Mix everything with the Nutella.
8. Add the whipped cream then the whites to snow.
9. Let turbinate 20 to 30 minutes, and its ready!

Nutritional Information

- Total Carbohydrate 16 g   5%
- Dietary fiber 0.6 g   2%
- Sugar 15 g
- Protein 4.1 g   8%
- Caffeine 7 mg
- Vitamin A   10%
- Vitamin C   0%
- Calcium   9%
- Iron   3%
- Vitamin B-6   5%
- Cobalamin   8%
- Magnesium   5%

Watermelons Fruit Sushi

Cooking time: 30 to 60 min

Ingredients

Servings: 10

- 1 piece of watermelon (should be enough for 20 slices of 5 x 2.5 cm)
- 1 piece of lemon (juice of it)
- 10 g of sugar
- Basil leaves (fresh or dried)
- 1/2 serving of lemon rice

Preparation

1. For the watermelon Fruit sushi, cut the watermelon into thin slices and marinate for five to ten minutes in the mixture of lemon juice and sugar.
2. Place the melon slices on a baking sheet lined with baking paper and place them in the air fryer under the grill until they are lightly browned on the surface.
3. Of lemon rice form and put on it the melon slices with the grilled side

down. Sprinkle with a pinch of chopped basil and serve the watermelon Fruit sushi.

Tip

After a few minutes under the grill, the watermelon gets a very special color and texture, which reminds a bit of tuna. If you have guests, let them try and guess what's on the fruit sushi before you reveal the secret of the watermelon Fruit sushi.

Nutritional Information

- Calories 30
- Total Fat 0.2 g
- Saturated fat 0 g
- Polyunsaturated fat 0.1 g
- Monounsaturated fat 0 g
- Cholesterol 0 mg
- Sodium 1 mg
- Potassium 112 mg
- Total Carbohydrate 8 g
- Dietary fiber 0.4 g
- Sugar 6 g
- Protein 0.6 g
- Vitamin A   11%

- Vitamin C   13%
- Calcium   0%
- Coalmine   0%
- Magnesium   2%

Milk with Strawberry Coulis

Ingredients (4 people)

- 2 tablespoons icing sugar
- 100g of strawberry
- 50 cl of milk

Preparation

1. Rinse the strawberries with fresh water and strain them in a colander, remove the tails from the strawberries.
2. Place the strawberries and icing sugar in the blender jar and finely mix everything in a grout.
3. Spread the strawberry coulis in the glasses.

4. Pour the milk gently into the glasses and serve immediately.
5. Enjoy your meal!

Nutritional Information

- Carbs 42 g
- Dietary Fiber 1 g
- Sugar12 g
- Fat24 g
- Saturated11 g
- Polyunsaturated0 g
- Protein6 g
- Sodium395 mg

Asparagus and trout salad

Excellent as a starter or main dish if you double the quantities.

4 people

Preparation time: 10 min.

Ingredients

400 g green asparagus

400 g raw skinless trout

40 g spring onions

100 g of young shoots (purslane, spinach...)

1 tablespoon (s) of caper flower

Vinaigrette

5 tablespoon (s) of olive oil

3 tablespoon (s) of apple cider vinegar

The juice of 1 lemon yellow

20 g spring onion whites

75 g capers

1/2 teaspoon (s) of salt

Preparation

1. Rinse and cut each asparagus lengthwise with a peeler to obtain strips. Place them in a colander and pour 2 l of boiling water over them, then immediately place them for 5 minutes in very cold water so that they retain a beautiful green color. Drain and set aside.

2. Cut the fish into 1 cm cubes.

3. Cut the green part of the onions into thin strips and soak them in water for a few minutes. Slice the white part and set aside.

4. Mix all ingredients for the dressing and mix in the blender.

5. Put the asparagus, the young shoots, and the white of the onions, the caper flowers

and the raw fish in a bowl. Season with vinaigrette.

Armand Arnal Arugula, Cucumber and Lisette

4 People

Preparation Time: 20 Min.

Ingredients

3 cucumbers

250 g arugula

2 spring onions

1 l vegetable broth

4 fillets of Lisette

4 cucumber flowers

1 bunch coriander

50 g salt

50 g sugar

50 cl olive oil

10 g coriander seeds

10 cl apple cider vinegar

Preparation

1. The day before: peel 1 diced cucumber, put in salt and olive oil. Vacuum leave in the fridge overnight.

2. D-Day: Cut the cucumbers into cubes, reserve

3. for the lisettes (which can be replaced by fresh sardines): lift the fillets, without the skin and remove the bones.

4. Mix salt, sugar and coriander seeds. Cover the fillets with this preparation, leave to stand for 10 min, then rinse with clear water and dry with absorbent paper. Put the fillets on the skin side in a bottom of apple cider vinegar for 10 min. extract the fine

skin. Cut the fillets into thin strips in the thickness direction. Reserve in a container with a little olive oil.

5. Cucumber water: Place the washed, unpeeled cucumbers and coriander in a centrifuge, season, refrigerate.

6. Arugula puree: Sweat the green of the spring onions, moisten with the vegetable broth. Remove the water, add the arugula then mix. Switch to Chinese, reserve.

7. Dressing: Arrange the arugula puree then a few diced cucumbers at the bottom of a bowl. Add the fillets of lisette. Decorate with a cucumber flower and a few coriander flowers. When serving, pour the cucumber water in the bowl.

Pumpkin seed Cheesecake

A hearty pumpkin seed cheesecake succeeds and tastes great and small. The recipe is prepared with curd cheese.

Ingredients for eight servings

- 100 G shortbread

- 30 G grated pumpkin seeds

- 80 G Flour

- 120 G Butter (room temperature)

- 30 ml pumpkin seed oil PGI

- 60 G icing sugar

- Three stick eggs

Ingredients for the abundance

- 500 G plugs

- 150 G sour cream

- 150 ml whipped cream

- 30 ml pumpkin seed oil PGI

- 180 G icing sugar

- 2 EL Flour

- 0.5 stick vanilla bean

Ingredients for the garnish

- Six stick strawberries

- One prize sugar

- One shot lemon juice

- One prize pumpkin seed brittle

- One shot of Woodruff or lemon balm

Preparation:

• Put the biscuits in the freezer and pound with a mallet. Pumpkin seeds, flour, pumpkin seed oil PGI, butter, icing sugar and knead.

- Butter a cake, fill with 3/4 of the mass and spread evenly with a spoon (press down a bit). Press a thin edge on the spring forming a wall with the remaining dough. Put the cake tin in the fridge for about 2 hours.

- For the filling, preheat the air fryer to 150 ° C. Stir cream, sugar, pumpkin seed oil, whipped cream and pith of vanilla pod until smooth. Add eggs and stir. Finally, fold in the flour.

- Distribute the filling evenly on the cooled soil in the spring form. Bake the cake at 150 ° C for 30 minutes, and then turn down the heat to 120 ° C and bake for another 15 minutes. Then turn off the air fryer. Let the cheesecake in it for an hour. Then cool and put in the fridge for two hours.

- Cut strawberries into small pieces, marinate with sugar and lemon juice. Distribute evenly on the cheesecake, sprinkle with pumpkin seed and icing sugar with Styria power.

Tips on the recipe

Garnish as desired with woodruff or lemon balm.

Nutritional Information:

- Kcal 439

- Kj 1842

- Protein 16 G

- Fat 7 G

- Carbohydrates 76 g

Soup 'green
Quantity: 1 person

Preparation: 15 minutes

Refrigeration: 15 minutes (optional)

Ingredients:

Water in sufficient quantity to achieve the desired texture

1 green apple with skin

1 slice of fresh peeled ginger

Half lemon or 1 lime without skin, the white part without seeds

Half cucumber with skin

Half bowl of leaves with fresh spinach

1 bunch of basil or fresh cilantro

1 branch of wireless celery, including tender green leaves

Preparation:

1. Wash and chop all the ingredients. Insert them into the glass of blender and crush.

2. Add the water and crush again until you get a homogeneous texture. If necessary, rectify water.

3. Take the soup as a snack at any time of the day to purify the body and keep cravings at bay. To know more: This cold soup is quick to prepare and has great benefits for the body. Perhaps the best-known property of the apple is its intestinal regulatory action. If we eat it raw and with skin, it is useful to treat constipation, since this way we take advantage of its richness in insoluble fiber present in the skin, which stimulates the intestinal activity and helps to keep the intestinal muscles in shape. Also, green apples are one of the largest sources of flavonoids. These antioxidant compounds can stop the action of free radicals on the cells of the body. Eating raw fruits and vegetables is the healthiest option.

Nutritional Information

    Calories 330

    Fat 12 g 18 %

    Cholesterol 90 mg

Sodium 240 mg 10 %

Carbohydrate 20 g 6 %

Fibre 5 g 22 %

Sugars 4 g

Iron 15 %

Soup of noodles with vegetables
Quantity: 2 people

Preparation: 20 minutes

Cooking: 5 minutes

Ingredients:

2 liters of water

150 g of organic buckwheat noodles

2 cloves of garlic

1 laminated tender onion, including the tender green part

1 laminated leek

1 carrot cut in julienne

5 or 6 laminated mushrooms

1 trunk of celery, cut into thin slices

Half red pepper

Half green pepper

1 tbsp. fresh ginger

1 strip of wakame seaweed

1 pinch of sea salt

Ground black pepper

Extra virgin olive oil

Soy sauce

Parsley and chopped fresh chives sprinkle

Preparation:

1. In a pot with a lid, heat a tablespoon of oil and sauté the garlic, onion, and leek over medium heat.

2. Add the carrot, mushrooms, celery, and red and green pepper cut into thin strips, the freshly grated ginger, and the seaweed. Cover and sauté 3 to 4 minutes with the pot

covered. If necessary add some tablespoon of water to facilitate cooking.

3. Salt, cover with water and boil on low heat for about 5 minutes.

4. In a separate pot, bring two liters of boiling water and boil the noodles (follow the package instructions).

5. Drain, immediately pour a small number of noodles into a bowl and add the broth with the vegetables.

6. Season with a string of soy sauce, sprinkle with the herbs and dress with a string of olive oil. Serves hot

Nutritional Information

Calories 159

% Daily Value

6%Total Fat 3.8g grams

9%Total Carbohydrates 26g grams

Sugars 4g grams

Protein 5.8g

Dry belly soup with cabbage and celery

The ingredients have the function of detoxifying the body, eliminating excess swelling and retention of liquid. Celery is diuretic, the onion has the function of detoxifying, the cabbage has low calories and improves bowel function, and the bell peppers bring satiety and more fiber to the body.

Ingredients:

1/2 chopped cabbage

6 large chopped onions

6 tomatoes chopped without seeds

3 stalks of celery

2 green peppers

Salt to taste

Pepper to taste

Oregano to taste

Preparation:

1. Wash vegetables and chop as instructed above. Bring all of these

ingredients into a pan with water to cover.
2. Let it cook over medium-high heat with the pan semi-capped.
3. Season with salt, pepper and oregano and other spices and herbs you prefer.
4. Cook until the vegetables are tender. Serve immediately.

Nutritional Information

Calories: 165.2

Sugars: 4.1 g

Dietary Fiber: 12.0 g

Total Fat: 1.8 g

Chicken soup

Ingredients:

1 tablespoon coconut oil

1 sliced organic yellow onion

3 grated carrots

2 chopped celery

2 cloves garlic, crushed

1 tablespoon curry powder

8 cups low-sodium chicken broth

3 cups chopped roasted chicken

1 bay leaf

1 sliced organic apple

1 pinch of pepper

½ teaspoon dried thyme

Shavings of a lemon

2 cups unsweetened coconut milk

1 pinch of salt

Preparation:

1. Place the coconut oil inside a large saucepan with medium heat. After this, add the onion, celery, and carrot to cook, stirring occasionally for five minutes.
2. Then add the garlic cloves and curry powder and cook for another two minutes.

3. Add the chicken broth, chicken, bay leaf, apple, pepper, thyme, and lemon zest and stir well. Simmer for another 40 minutes.
4. Then mix with the coconut milk and salt. Remove the bay leaf and serve.

Nutritional Information

Calories 36   % Daily Value

Total Fat 1.2 g   1%

Saturated fat 0.3 g 1%

Polyunsaturated fat 0.2 g

Monounsaturated fat 0.6 g

Cholesterol 3 mg   1%

Sodium 143 mg   5%

Potassium 105 mg 3%

Total Carbohydrate 3.5 g 1%

Dietary fiber 0 g   0%

Sugar 1.6 g

Protein 2.5 g   5%

Tomato and garlic soup
Quantity: 2 people

Preparation: 40 minutes

Cooking: 20 minutes

Ingredients:

Half a liter of water

1 purple onion, thinly sliced

8-10 cloves of garlic rolled

1 kilo of ripe tomatoes, without skin

2 or 3 bay leaves

1 pinch of cayenne pepper, optional for a spicier touch

1 pinch of black pepper

Sea salt, to taste

1 tsp. Provencal herbs

1 pinch of cumin to it sprinkle

Extra virgin olive oil

Preparation:

1. In a pot, sauté the onion and garlic in 1 tablespoon of olive oil. Remove often, so they do not burn.

2. Blanch the tomatoes into boiling water, remove the skin and, if you prefer, also the seeds.

3. Add to the pot the tomatoes cut in quarters and the rest of the ingredients. Remove and cook over low heat for 10 minutes and with the pot covered, until the tomato acquires a slightly orange tone.

4. Add the water, and boil for about 10 minutes.

5. Remove the bay leaves and crush until you get a light texture. If necessary, add more water and rectify salt.

6. Serve the hot soup dressed with a strand of extra virgin olive oil and sprinkled with the cumin. To learn more: "Help fight infections with the antibiotic power of garlic," explains nutritionist Llargués. It has traditionally been used to prevent infections. Its flavor is dominant, compensated in this recipe by the tomato.

Nutritional Information

Calories: 81.3

Total Fat: 2.1 g

Dietary Fiber: 2.7 g

Saturated Fat: 1.1 g

Lettuce Tacos with Chicken to the Shepherd

Preparation time: 1 h 20 minutes

Cooking time: 35 minutes

<u>Ingredients</u>

6 Servings

50 grams of achiote for the marinade

1/4 cup of apple vinegar for the marinade

3 pieces of clean guajillo chile, deveined and seedless, hydrated for the marinade

2 pieces of wide chili, deveined and seedless, hydrated for the marinade

3 garlic cloves for the marinade

1/4 piece of white onion for the marinade

1/2 cup pineapple juice for marinade

1 tablespoon salt marinade

1 tablespoon fat pepper for marinade

2 pieces of clove for the marinade

1 tablespoon oregano for the marinade

1 piece of roasted guaje tomato, for the marinade

1 tablespoon cumin for the marinade

1 piece of boneless and skinless chicken breast, cut into small cubes

1 tablespoon of olive or flax oil

Enough of French Lettuce Eva

1/2 piece of pineapple cut into half moons

1/2 cup chopped coriander

1/2 cup finely chopped purple onion

To the taste of tree chili sauce to accompany

To the taste of lemon to accompany

Preparation

1.   For the marinade, blend the vinegar, chilies, garlic, onion, achiote, juice, salt, oregano, tomato, pepper, cloves, and cumin till a homogeneous mixture is obtained.

2.   Put the chicken and the marinade inside a bowl with the shepherd marinade for 1 hour in refrigeration.

3.   Heat a pan over medium temperature with the oil and cook the chicken you marinated until it is cooked. Reserve covered.

4.   Heat a grill over immense heat, roast the pineapple until golden brown, remove and cut into cubes, reserve.

5.   On a table place sheets of French Lettuce Eva, put the chicken to the shepherd and serve with the roasted pineapple, cilantro, onion, served with a little sauce and lemons.

Nutritional information

Calories   92.2   kcal 4.6%

Carbohydrates   22.3   g 7.4%

Proteins   1.6   g 3.2%

Dietary fiber   2.9   g 5.8%

Sugars   6.6   g 7.4%

Apple Green Ceviche

Preparation time: 10 minutes

Cooking time: 20 minutes

<u>Ingredients</u>

3 Servings

- 1/4 cup of lemon juice

- 1/3 cup of orange juice

- 2 tablespoons of olive oil

- 1/4 bunch of cilantro

- 2 pieces of green apple without peel, cut into medium cubes

- 1 piece of finely chopped serrano chili

- 1 cup of jicama cut into medium cubes

- 1 piece of avocado cut into cubes

1 cup cucumber cut into cubes

1/4 bunch of finely chopped basil leaf

1/4 cup of finely chopped cilantro

1 pinch of salt

1 piece of sliced radish

1 piece of serrano chili cut into slices

1/4 piece of purple onion

Preparation

4. Add lemon juice, orange juice, olive oil and cilantro to the blender. Blend perfectly well. Reservation.
5. Add to a bowl the apple, serrano pepper, jicama, avocado, cucumber, basil, cilantro, mix with the preparation of the blender and season perfectly well.
6. Serve the ceviche in a deep dish and decorate with the radish the chile serrano and the purple onion. Enjoy

Nutritional information

Calories   61.9   kcal 3.1%

Carbohydrates   14.4   g 4.8%

Proteins   1.6   g 3.1%

Lipids   0.3   g 0.4%

Dietary fiber   5.1   g 10%

Sugars   6.2   g 6.9%

Cholesterol   0.0   mg 0.0%

Blue hawaii
Ingredients

Lemonade (soda, sprite, 7up)

6 cl of pineapple juice

4 cl white rum

2 cl cane sugar syrup

2 cl blue curaçao

1 lemon juice

Utensils

1 mixing glass

Preparation

Make the recipe "Blue hawaii" in a mixing glass.

In the mixing glass. Serve in a tumbler. Fill with soda.

Serve in a tumbler glass.

No decoration.

Dry belly soup recipe with sweet potato

Ingredients:

1 tablespoon of olive oil;

2 cloves garlic, minced;

1 medium chopped onion;

3 tomatoes skinless and chopped seeds;

2 chopped zucchini;

1 medium sweet potato chopped;

2 cups chopped spinach

Chopped parsley to taste

1 liter of water

Salt to taste

Preparation:

1. Inside a saucepan, heat the olive oil and then sauté the garlic, onion, and tomato.
2. Add zucchini, peeled and chopped sweet potatoes and spinach and cook for 5 minutes. Add water, salt and cook until tender.
3. Wait for the soup to simmer and beat in the blender until you get a creamy soup.
4. Return to the pot to heat, season seasoning if necessary and serve with fresh parsley.

Nutrition Information

Dietary Fiber: 2.6 g

Protein: 3.2 g

Calories: 132.5

Total Fat: 5.3 g

Pumpkin Soup

In addition to having just 144 calories and rendering four servings, this recipe for weight-loss soup brings the pumpkin, which is rich in fiber, thus providing a sense of satiety to the body.

Ingredients:

2 chuchus

1 medium slice of tomato

½ small onions

2 garlic cloves

½ plates (table) of Swiss chard

1 stalk of celery

1 tablespoon chopped parsley

4 small pieces of pumpkin

- ❖ 2 ½ cups of water
- ❖ 1 teaspoon light salt
- ❖ Pepper to taste
- ❖ 1 plate (table) of endive
- ❖ 2 egg whites

Preparation:

1. Peel and chop all ingredients, except eggs.
2. Put the ingredients in a saucepan, except the endive. Add water, salt, and pepper.
3. Cook until soft, turn off the heat and beat in the blender until a homogeneous mixture is obtained.
4. Add in a saucepan the broth, finely chopped endive strips and whipped whites. Cook a little more, turn off the heat and serve.

Nutritional Information

Protein: 10.1 g

Calories: 164.8

Sodium: 1,060.4 mg

Total Carbohydrate: 22.7 g

Dry Soup Recipe for Pumpkin Belly

Being a source of fiber, the pumpkin helps to cause a feeling of satiety avoiding excessive consumption. Also, the pumpkin is low calorie: 100 grams contains only 40 calories. Make use of this ingredient to lose weight. Ginger helps to speed up metabolism by being thermogenic.

Ingredients:

1/2 Japanese Pumpkin

0.19 inch ginger, without chopped peel

1 chopped onion

3 cloves garlic, crushed

3 stalks of holy grass

1 1/2 l of water

Olive oil to taste

Preparation

1. Wash the pumpkin in running water. In a pan, put 2 cups water, the pumpkin and lightly cook over medium heat for 10 minutes.
2. Meanwhile, wash, peel and slice the ginger. Peel garlic and onion cut the onion into 4 parts.

3. Transfer pre-cooked squash to a board and, with the vegetable peeler, remove the peel. Reserve the cooking water. Cut the pumpkin into cubes and return to the pan with the water. Add the ginger, the garlic, the onion, the holy grass and the rest of the water. Bring to the medium heat and cook with the pan covered for 40 minutes.
4. After this time, remove the stalks of holy grass. Transfer to the blender and beat everything. Season with little salt and pepper to taste return the soup to the pan to heat and serve them.

Nutrition Information

Total Carbohydrate   16.1 g

Dietary Fiber   4.6 g

Sugars 5.9 g

Protein 7.2 g

Zucchini and basil soup

Ingredients for 4 persons:

1 kg zucchini

1 large potato

1 handful of fresh basil leaves

1 onion

2 cloves garlic

olive oil

salt

pepper

Preparation:

Peel and mince the onion.

Peel the potato then cut it into cubes.

Cut the zucchini into small cubes without peeling them.

Heat 3 tbsp. oil in a casserole plate and brown the onions.

When the onions are melted add the diced zucchini and potatoes.

Peel off garlic cloves and crush them with the handle of a knife to bring out the aromas, add them to the casserole dish.

Salt, pepper and cover with 30cl of water.

Close the casserole dish and simmer over low heat for about 40 minutes. (15 min. For a pressure cooker).

When the zucchini is cooked, add the basil leaves and mix everything. Adjust seasoning.

Serve warm or cold.

Tropical Smoothie

Ingredients:

½ mango

100 grams of pineapple

3 stems bok choy

100 ml unsweetened coconut milk

100 ml of water

6 tips and 1 warning

To conclude, read here our 6 best tips for the starting green smoothie maker. Do not forget the very last warning if you want to lose weight with smoothies!

1. Vary!

Make a smoothie every day with different types of vegetables, fruit, nuts and seeds. Variation is the magic word if you want to stay healthy and young.

2. Make sure you always have a bag or sprout of green leafy vegetables in your home.

Think of a bag of endive, kale, lettuce or spinach. If necessary, freeze it so that you are sure that you will never miss it.

3. Smoothie failed? That's how you save him!

Add one of these ingredients to save a failed smoothie: ½ banana, piece of avocado or teaspoon of (raw) honey. You can include a tablespoon of protein powder (natural or sweetened with pure stevia).

4. Add ice cubes

This makes your smoothie nice and cool! You can also make a cold smoothie by following the following tip.

5. Use frozen fruit

Cut ripe fruit into pieces, put it in a plastic bag or container and place it in the freezer. Frozen banana fits perfectly in a green smoothie; this gives the smoothie a delicious soft ice cream-like structure. You can also buy ready-made packages of frozen fruit in the supermarket. This is also a lot cheaper than fresh fruit, and contains just as many vitamins.

6. You can always replace unsweetened almond milk with water

Do you not have any almond milk in the house? Then you can simply add water. The smoothie may be less creamy, but it still has a delicious taste!

Warning: do not use too much fruit

Fruit is healthy, but also contains a lot of carbohydrates. These can stand in the way of losing weight. Use 1 to 1.5 servings of fruit in your smoothie. This can be: 1 banana + a handful of berries, or 1 pear + a small peach. With this amount of fruit you know for sure that you will never get too many carbohydrates.

Grouper in green sauce

A soft and delicious low-calorie fish easy to prepare and serve in green tomatillo sauce

Yield: 2 servings

Ingredients

- ➤ 2 grouper fillets
- ➤ Salt and pepper
- ➤ 1 tablespoon of olive oil

For the sauce:

- ➤ 2 tomatillos, without the peel
- ➤ ¼ cup of pumpkin seeds
- ➤ ½ cup of green paprika, without seeds or veins
- ➤ ½ cup of coriander leaves only
- ➤ ½ of a jalapeño, without seeds or veins
- ➤ ½ cup of parsley leaves only
- ➤ ½ teaspoon fresh thyme
- ➤ 3 garlic cloves
- ➤ ¼ cup of fish stock
- ➤ 1 pinch of salt

Preparation:

1. In a medium saucepan with water at the time, add the tomatillos and boil 1 minute. Stir and place in the blender.
2. In a medium skillet, add the seeds and toast on low, medium heat for 1

to 2 minutes or until golden brown. Remove and place in the blender.

3. Pour the rest of the ingredients. Blend well.

4. Pour out the sauce into the pan and then cook over medium heat for 1 minute.

5. Dry the fish fillets with the paper towel and salt and pepper to taste.

6. In another wide pan, add the olive oil and let it heat over medium-high heat.

7. Place the steaks and let them brown, 3 to 4 minutes on each side. Serve with the sauce.

Tart apple and carrots soup

Ingredients

- ➤ 800 g carrots
- ➤ 2 golden apples
- ➤ 1 onion
- ➤ 1.5 liters of water
- ➤ 1 cubic broth of vegetables preferably
- ➤ Ginger
- ➤ Salt pepper

Preparation

1. Wash and peel the carrots and apples, cut into small pieces.
2. Cut the onion and sweat it in a pan with oil.
3. Add carrots and apples.
4. In a saucepan, melt the cubed vegetable broth in 1.5 liters of water.
5. Cover the vegetables with the broth.
6. Season and boil for 30 minutes.
7. Mix everything together.

Black bean and avocado soup

Ingredients

Servings: 10

> - 1 can (540 ml) of black beans, drained
> - 1 can (398 ml) corn kernels, drained
> - 4 roma tomatoes, seeded and chopped
> - 1 red pepper, diced
> - 1 jalapeno pepper, chopped
> - 1/3 cup chopped fresh cilantro
> - 1/4 cup red onion
> - 1/4 cup fresh lime juice
> - 2 tbsp. Red wine vinegar
> - 1 c. Salt
> - 1/2 c. Pepper
> - 2 lawyers, diced

Preparations

Combine all ingredients except avocados inside a big bowl and mix. Add the avocados and mix gently. Cover with plastic wrap (directly on the salsa) and refrigerate at least 2 hours before serving.

Cream of pear and arugula

Quantity: 2 Persians

Preparation: 20 minutes

Cooling: 15-20 minutes

Ingredients:

Half a liter of water

4 pears blanquillos with leather, at its point of maturation

1 bowl of arugula

2 tablespoons of fresh aromatic herbs

The juice of 1 small lemon

Sea salt or herbal salt

1 pinch of ground black pepper

Extra virgin olive oil

Edible flowers to decorate

Preparation:

1. Grind whole the ingredients in the blender jar, except extra virgin olive oil and flowers, until a creamy and homogeneous texture is obtained. If necessary, rectify water, salt, and pepper.

2. Refrigerate until ready to serve and, once in the bowl, decorate with the flowers and a thread of olive oil. If you do not have flowers, then you can use chopped almonds, some rocket leaves or sesame seeds.

3. If you do not have a bowl of arugula you can also use other green leaves such as spinach, lamb's lettuce, watercress, mustard greens, etc. with the aromatic herbs, the same: you can make with parsley, dill, chives, basil, cilantro or mint. To know more: The pear is a fruit with satiating effect for its fiber content: it is fantastic for people who want to lose weight and are doing a diet to lose weight. Also, it is a fruit with anti-inflammatory action, helps us maintain a regular intestinal transit and combat constipation, and has a very beneficial effect

on our microbiota or intestinal flora. Choose it whenever you can from organic farming.

Nutritional Information

Calories   197.1

Total Fat   12.1 g

Saturated Fat   3.2 g

Polyunsaturated Fat   3.5 g

Monounsaturated Fat   4.1 g

Cholesterol   10.0 mg

Sodium   181.2 mg

Potassium 149.7 mg

Total Carbohydrate   21.3 g

Dietary Fiber   3.0 g

Sugars   15.9 g

Protein   3.5 g

Baked Sea Bream In Lebanese Style
Preparation: 10 mins

Cooking Time: 40 mins

Number of Serving: 2-3 persons

Ingredients:

For the dish:

- ✓ 1 kilogram of whole fish type bream, salmon or trout
- ✓ 1 teaspoon of salt
- ✓ 1 teaspoon of cumin
- ✓ 1 teaspoon sweet pepper (paprikas)
- ✓ 1 onion
- ✓ 1 lemon
- ✓ 2 bay leaves
- ✓ 3 tomatoes

For the sauce:

- ✓ 3 cloves of garlic
- ✓ 1 tablespoon coriander seeds
- ✓ 1/2 teaspoon of salt
- ✓ 100 g of onion
- ✓ 1/2 bunch of green coriander

- ✓ 65 g of tahini (sesame puree)
- ✓ 1 lemon or about 50 ml of lemon juice
- ✓ 1/2 glass of vegetable oil (sunflower or olive)
- ✓ 10 g pine nuts
- ✓ 25 g chopped walnuts
- ✓ 1/2 to 1 teaspoon of fine cayenne pepper powder (according to taste)
- ✓ 1 pinch of pepper

Preparation:

1. Wash the fish; rub both sides with a teaspoon of salt, sweet pepper, and cumin. In a big baking tray, add onion, tomatoes, and lemon sliced and put the fish and bay leaf. Add 1 glass of water. Sprinkle with a drizzle of olive oil.

2. Heat up the oven to 180 ° C. Put the tray in the oven and cook for 20 minutes or 25 minutes depending on the type and thickness of the fish.

3. With a pestle, crush garlic, salt, and coriander seeds until coriander becomes powder. Set aside.

4. Minute an onion, finely chop green coriander and leave aside.

5. In a large bowl, pour tahini, lemon juice, and 100 ml water. Mix well until you obtain a homogeneous liquid, then reserve.

6. In a saucepan, add vegetable oil, heat over medium heat. Brown the pine nuts, drain them.

7. In the same saucepan and remaining oil, brown the chopped onion. Add green coriander, the garlic-cilantro mixture in seeds and chopped walnuts and pepper. Simmer another 10 minutes. Finally, add tahini, lemon, and water. Cook for about 10 minutes.

8. Add the chili, mix and remove from the heat. Leave this sauce aside for dressing.

To serve, place the fish on a large plate, decorate with slices of peppers, tomatoes or any other vegetable to give color. Put the

sauce on the fish, and then scatter over the
pine nuts.

Good realization and good tasting!

Nutritional Information

Potassium 967.12mg   28%

Carbohydrates 0g   0%

Dietary Fiber 0g   0%

Sugars 0g

Simpler Way To Lose Weight

As a result of diets with very low calories, a diet based on diet or protein-based diets, you quickly lose the weight you want, but you are doomed to gain more weight after a certain period of time.

You find yourself in a very familiar vicious circle, right?

It is getting challenging to lose weight in this vicious circle, and your hopes are running out for losing weight every day. Because the problem is not in the diets applied, but in your lifestyle!

The only way to improve your lifestyle is to permanently lose the weight you have gained over the years. Although it is not easy to achieve this, you can start by following these 18 tips.

Set realistic goals

Like many people who want to lose weight, they often start dieting, but after a while, you have trouble adjusting the diet program because you do not set realistic goals for yourself in the weight loss process.

When setting out on this path, you should first set yourself a realistic weight goal. This target will always be your guide while motivating you while dieting.

Maybe you also thought about setting realistic goals. So what's really realistic?

It is best to set a goal of losing 0.5-1 pound a week in the long run. As a result of the wrong diets applied, you may have lost more weight in a week. Losing weight once a week may not make you happy, but those weights you will lose will be permanent for a long time. You can permanently get rid of your 12 pounds after three months by losing 1 kilo a week.

Remember, losing the weight you gain in a long time gradually but surely will completely save you from this trouble.

Keep Your Motivation High

"Tomorrow, Monday, next week, after the holidays, I am starting a holiday return diet!" Who knows how many times you made this promise to yourself?

Even the most disciplined people can give up when it comes to weakening or change their mind soon.

Even if your logic says, "Okay, now I will get rid of my extra pounds / go to a healthier life," your inner conversations will resist, "I will never succeed / or again, will I struggle in vain?" Usually, we are always defeated because our inner speeches are mentioned.

To get rid of this cycle, you must keep your motivation high.

The advice for this is not to postpone your decision.

Once you start, remember why you started to maintain your determination. Please note that this process is very difficult at the beginning, but it becomes more enjoyable as time goes on.

So keep in mind that the more patient you are, the more successful you will be. Managing to keep yourself motivated will separate you from unsuccessful people.

Try to find ideas to motivate yourself. Maybe you can consider your clothes, which you loved before but are no longer for you, hang the old pictures that you are more fit and healthy on the refrigerator, and focus yourself on your goal.

Do Not neglect to drink water

Water is a magic drink that allows you to lose weight.

Water provides the functioning of our body's metabolism, closes appetite, and is effective in burning fat.

Water with numerous benefits is a natural appetizer and effective in breaking stored fat in the body. Studies show that people with reduced water consumption increase their fat stores.

It is recommended to consume 1 ml per calorie we take daily or 35 ml of water per 1 kg if we set off from the weight of the person. The World Health Organization reports that women should drink ten glasses of water a day and men drink 14 glasses a day to prevent fluid loss.

Even though the coffee, tea, and juices we drink during the day seem to meet the person's fluid need, these drinks increase the water excretion from the body. For this reason, when we consume diuretic drinks such as tea and coffee, we need to drink more water.

Those who forget to drink water will provide their water consumption if they need to drink water hourly. Likewise, carrying our water with us while working in the office and walking on the street will have a positive effect on water consumption.

3-4 cinnamon sticks, a few sliced apple and lemon slices you will throw into your bottle or jug, you can flavor your water and provide a different way of drinking.

Avoid shock diets

As a general rule, you should stay away from diets that lose weight fast. The reason is simple: You cannot lose the weight you have gained over the years.

Although these diets lose weight fast, the weight loss is not from fat, but from muscle and water. Therefore, when your body returns to normal, you will recover these pounds, and you will be open to gaining more weight as your muscle mass decreases.

This is the reason for the rapid weight gain after the diets.

Another disadvantage of these diets is that they will starve your body. If you stay hungry during the day, your blood sugar drops, you may experience weakness, weakness, fatigue, and fainting. Your work efficiency decreases, and you observe a decrease in the ability to understand and learn. This situation causes your quality of life to decrease and your body's resistance to fall and gain more weight.

Another negative effect of shock diets is slowing metabolism. With such diets, metabolism slows down as muscle tissue is lost rather than fat tissue. Some weight is lost, but they are taken back at the first opportunity. Even if the person eats less or as much as before, he continues to gain weight. Later on, diets made it difficult to lose weight.

All you have to do is to stay away from these diets, turn to healthier methods, and work with a professional.

Don't start the day without breakfast

The first condition to start the day should be breakfast for those who want to lose weight. Many researches are about having regular breakfast; It shows that it lowers cholesterol, breaks insulin resistance, and positively affects physical performance.

Having regular breakfast also has an effect on weight control. Harvard researchers; followed a group of patients for ten years. As a result of the research, they stated that those who did not eat breakfast gained 11 kilos compared to those who had breakfast.

In addition, individuals who eat breakfast regularly do not have vitamin and mineral deficiencies, and individuals who prefer to sleep in the morning lose weight faster and face a risk of a heart attack.

Bypassing breakfast, you tend to consume more fat and carbohydrate foods without lunch. In this case, it causes more energy intake than necessary and an increase in weight in the future.

An accurate breakfast can include eggs, cheese, whole grain bread, olives and honey, jam, butter, or bagels, depending on the person's energy needs. Or a lean toast or cold sandwich prepared with whole grain bread. But not a donut!

Usually, a choice for a rush breakfast is a pastry and never 1 of them. But with only one bun, we meet about 1/4 of our daily energy needs. In other words, a donut contains approximately 300 - 400 calories and 20 grams of fat. It doesn't sound very innocent when you say that, right?

When you have breakfast quickly, whole grain cereals, muesli and oatmeal are the healthiest saviors.

By adding about 4 tablespoons of oatmeal and fresh or dried fruit to 1 cup of semi-skimmed milk, you start your day with a meal that you will prepare in less than 5 minutes, and you make a healthy choice.

Pay attention to emotional hunger

Have you ever noticed that you are eating for your emotions, not for your stomach?

Emotional hunger is a big problem today and can often be confused with physical hunger. In other words, hunger, which is felt even when the body does not need it, causes more consumption and increases weight.

The most logical way to get rid of this situation is to distinguish these two types of hunger.

So how do we differentiate emotional hunger and physical hunger?

Physical hunger does not start suddenly, a feeling of hunger gradually occurs, but a feeling of hunger in emotional hunger appears suddenly. You feel that you need to suppress emotional hunger at once, but physical hunger can wait. If you eat to fill your emotional emptiness, you will continue to eat even if your stomach is full. On the other hand, if you're really hungry, you stop eating when your stomach is full.

The first step to stop emotional hunger is to stop and ask yourself if you are really hungry. If the answer to this question is no, then it is necessary to drink a glass of water. On the other hand, if the answer to this question is yes, wait, and evaluate how hungry you are.

Distracting your mind helps you overcome emotional hunger. To do this, you can call your friend to chat, go out, or take care of a hobby. Of course, you can watch a movie or listen to music without popcorn.

Eat a snack

Apart from the main meals, the snack is a type of meal that is made at certain and regular hours and consists of healthy foods that are not very high energy.

Making snacks is one of the most important tricks for losing weight. Having a snack in the diet helps control blood sugar, accelerate metabolism, and increase fat burning. The snack also provides a feeling of fullness, making it easier to control portions of main meals and supplements the missing nutrients.

Healthy snack recommendations:

- Skim milk + one serving of fruit

- 1 whole wheat toast + herbal tea

- Skimmed milk coffee + 1 dried apricot

- 2 walnuts + 1 serving of fruit

Keeping the snacks you will consume in your bag, in your car's eye, or in the office drawer will prevent you from skipping meals and consuming unhealthy and weight-saving alternative foods.

Act at work

Working life means immobility for many people.

Since less physical effort is spent in office environments, protein losses and increases in fat mass occur after a certain period of time, even without weight gain. So it is very important to act.

Create excuses for yourself to increase movement in the office. For example, instead of using an elevator, choose the stairs, prepare your own food if you have the atmosphere, get up every hour and make it a habit to walk for two or three minutes.

If you are going to work near a place outside of work, walk if possible. If you are heading to a distant place, you can get off a few stops and walk to the destination.

Eat fruit instead of junk food

If you aim to lose weight, you have to cut the junk food!

Unhealthy snacks such as fast food, sugar, chocolate, ice cream, chips, coke cause you to never lose weight.

But we also need to meet our appetite for snacking. For this, fruits are the ideal solution. Because fruits contain high levels of fiber, vitamins, and minerals; It not only cuts your stomach and wants to snack, but also keeps it full for a long time.

The only thing you need to pay attention to is the portions. Although healthy, some fruits contain more sugar than others. So you can accept and consume a handful of fruit.

Shop for a healthy kitchen

Healthy eating begins in shopping. Whatever you buy, you consume it at home. So you have to be very careful about shopping.

Preparing a shopping list is the easiest and critical step in this matter. Making a list in advance prevents you from spending unnecessary and getting plenty of calorie foods.

I prefer fresh vegetables and fruits instead of buying packaged products.

Since the additives are low in natural foods, the "Ingredients" list will be plain. Do not choose foods that are too full of ingredients.

If you buy the same foods in every purchase, you will not be able to make the changes you want, and you will not be able to provide a variety of foods. From time to time, choose different options from the same food group.

Instead of over-fat and over-salty foods, buy foods with reduced fat and salt content.

Get to know the foods you take; Be sure to read the label information, production and expiration dates, and nutrient content section. Compare the foods that are similar to each other and put the most nutritious in your basket.

Finally, be careful not to be hungry while shopping. Do not forget that going shopping when you are hungry increases the amount of shopping and fills the basket with unhealthy foods.

Eat Dairy

Foods in milk and milk products such as yogurt, buttermilk, and kefir are an important source of calcium, phosphorus, protein, B2, B12, and vitamin D. These minerals are essential for losing weight. Consuming them less causes the body to store fatter.

For example, calcium is one of the essential minerals found in milk and dairy products. Research shows that adequate calcium intake is easier to lose weight.

The daily calcium need of adult individuals is about 1000 milligrams. One can comfortably provide the daily need for calcium by consuming 2-3 glasses of milk and dairy products and help to weaken.

When low-fat dairy products are compared with full-fat products, their calcium content does not change. Turning to low-fat sources of calcium also helps in maintaining weight control. It is advised to take in low-fat dairy products in weight loss programs.

Research shows that milk and dairy products in diets of overweight individuals are a good control providers and effectively decrease insulin resistance.

Take a Walk

Walking is an exercise that can be done easily anytime and anywhere. Regular walks will help you lose weight quickly and help maintain physical and mental health.

At the beginning of the walk, the body uses glycogen first. With a decrease in the amount of glycogen in the blood, the brain stops glycogen use and begins to break down fat in the body. On the other hand, the muscles' oxygen requirement increases; at this point, the speed of the walk is important to carry oxygen to the muscles.

To ensure that the body burns fat, walking should be done briskly and with plenty of breathing.

Approximately 400 calories can be burned from an average of 5-7 calories per minute with 1 hour of regular walking. This corresponds to an average of 6 - 7 kilos in a year. Since the body will start burning fat from 20 to 25 minutes, walking for 1 hour will speed up the weight loss process.

Eat Healthy Fats

One of the biggest mistakes made by those who want to lose weight is to stop consuming fat.

With a diet program without a fat group, people tend to consume more carbohydrates. In a healthy diet, approximately 30% of our daily energy needs should be provided from fats. Although it is thought to be high-calorie and avoided, oils are essential for keeping us full for longer.

Of course, you should be very careful while consuming oil, and the right oils should be consumed. The right oils are natural oils such as flaxseed, olive oil, raw almond oil, raw nuts, walnuts, avocado, sesame, coconut oil.

Fats to avoid are trans fats and margarine. This type of oil is often found in fast food products and is one of the main reasons for gaining weight.

Eat Whole Grain Bread

The first method that passes through the minds of people who decide to lose weight is to leave the bread. But like most known approaches, this is a mistake because our body needs carbohydrates and vitamins like B1.

But not all breads are of equal quality, just as in the same oils. While some types of bread make you gain more weight and don't have enough nutrition, others keep you full for longer and provide you with the vitamins, minerals, and carbohydrates you need.

White bread comes first among the types of bread that you should not consume. Because white bread raises your blood sugar fast due to the simple carbohydrates, it contains, so you get hungry quickly.

But the group called brown bread, like whole grain, rye, oat bread, keeps you full for a longer time and is more nutritious. Therefore, whole grain products are the most reliable, correct carbohydrate source in the slimming process.

Whole-grain breads help reduce weight by lowering your fat rate and prevent your metabolic rate from slowing down. In other words, these breads do not get fat, but rather help to weaken.

Pay Attention to Your Sleep Pattern

When it comes to losing weight, regular nutrition, a strict diet, and sports come to mind first. Regular sleep is often skipped. For a healthy life, regular nutrition, exercise, and sleep are equally important.

In people who sleep poorly, the level of the hormone leptin, which sends the saturation signal, decreases. This drop will cause you to eat later and eat more.

In some situations that cause stress in the body, such as insomnia, the level of hormone cortisol rises, and increased appetite is another negative effect of insomnia. Cortisol is a scientifically proven hormone that makes weight gain.

So you should pay attention to your sleep time and sleep quality. If possible, you should not get out of bed without having a complete rest. If you have trouble sleeping at night, you can take some precautions.

The main one of these measures is to prepare our body for sleep by consuming the right foods after dinner. These foods are; warm milk, yogurt, kefir, banana, apple, apricot, honey, flaxseed, and almond. You may prefer flaxseed yogurt or warm milk at your next meal after dinner.

Foods with huge caffeine content such as coffee, tea, and chocolate should not be consumed close to bedtime because caffeine has a sleeping effect. Especially in our country with high tea consumption, this problem is very common. Therefore, you will need to waive your tea after the evening during weight loss.

It is another precaution to stop eating until 2-3 hours before going to bed for quality sleep.

Shrink Your Portions

Portion control is the most effective way to lose weight without even realizing it. Because the more the portion sizes increase, the need to finish reflexively, and this habit causes us to consume more.

To prevent this situation, reducing the portions to a small extent allows you to lose more weight in the long run.

The best way to start in portion control is to use smaller plates. Thus, your plate will look fuller; you will reach the same saturation by eating less.

Another method is not to bring too much food to the table, if possible, not to cook it. Put the amount you need to eat on your plate in the kitchen and never put pots on the table. Even if you are saturated, if your favorite food is in front of you, you definitely want to finish it.

The same is true for fruits. I prefer small fruits instead of large ones (for example, take a small apple). If you are going to gain two kilos, reduce it to one and a half kilos.

When dieting, pay attention to the amount of food you eat and count it. For example; If you are going to consume nuts in the snack, do not make an eye decision. If the amount you need to eat is ten nuts, count it. This method will prevent you from getting unnecessary amounts of nutrients.

There is no magic diet, food, or medicine to lose weight. You cannot lose the weight you have gained over the years in a few days or weeks. All you ought to do is change your way of life and carefully live the rest of your life.

For this, you need to correct your nutrition and increase your movement. These changes are hard to accomplish in a day. You should keep your motivation high and make these items the way we live in the long run!

Healthy and Southern It is well documented that the Mediterranean diet keeps the heart doctor from the door. Build your diet around a high intake of olive oil, fruits, nuts, and vegetables. A moderate intake of fish and poultry, a low intake of dairy products, red meat, processed meat, and candy, and cake, optionally adds a glass of wine to the food. Stay away from. Cut down on the sugar. Too much sugar can increase the blood content of the so-called triglycerides found in the blood and lead to overweight. Two things that increase the likelihood of being affected by cardiovascular disease save on salt. Max. Six grams a day. Studies also show that high salt consumption over the long term can damage the heart's muscle and blood vessel function. Therefore, consuming a lot of salt is a risk factor for the development of cardiovascular disease regardless of age. Photo: Iris 8 Cut down on unsaturated fatty acids from meat.

Saturated fat can raise cholesterol levels and promote arteriosclerosis and blood clots. Keep working with processed foods and finished products again. They often contain a lot of salt and saturated fat, which helps increase the risk of getting cardiovascular disease. Inspiration Mediterranean food by Anne Skov gaard-Petersen: The book contains more than 140 recipes created in the south, but which can also be made at home. Dr. Hertz - Slim with Mediterranean food by Beagle Iuel-Brockdorff. General advice Eat at least 75 grams of dietary fiber a day. Whole grain products and coarse vegetables include rich in fibers that can help prevent cardiovascular disease. Fruits and vegetables are rich in vitamins, minerals, antioxidants that all protect you from cardiovascular disease. Eat at least 600 grams of fruit and vegetables a day. Eat at least 300 grams of fish a week. Vary between lean and fatty to get the essential omega-3 fatty acids. The fish include helps counteract high blood pressure and atherosclerosis. Fat from plant oils, nuts, and avocados are rich in healthy, unsaturated fat—the healthy fat decreases, among other things. Cholesterol levels and counteract atherosclerosis and blood clots. Therefore, be sure to supplement your diet daily with vegetable oil and nuts. The plate If you need to lose weight: Half the plate must be filled with vegetables, a quarter must be starch; potatoes and whole grain rice. The last quarter should be lean meat, poultry without skin, or fish—supplements with olive oil, nuts, or other foods with healthy fat. Y model: Meat, poultry, fish, cheese, and fat must be one-fifth of the total plate. Bread, coarse paste, or rice pasta should fill two-fifths of the plate. Vegetables - preferably coarse - and fruit should make up the last two-fifths of the plate.

Expert advice on a Mediterranean diet It is basically very simple to change one's diet to the Mediterranean diet. It just requires cutting meat consumption - and then eating some more vegetable oil and more vegetables. Plant foods such as onions, lettuce, tomato, cabbage, peas, beans, and peppers need to fill a great deal on the plate. The vegetables should be colorful as they are extra rich in beneficial antioxidants. At the same time, the food should not be lean. People in Crete were once the longest-lived population in the world - consuming up to 100 grams of olive oil a week. So there is no need to save on fat as long as you stay healthy. Eat lots of extra virgin olive oil and cold-pressed rapeseed oil in the food. At the same time, much of the recent research shows that butter is not as bad as you thought. Therefore, you do not necessarily have to hold back. Cut down on the amount of meat, especially the red streaks. Stick to poultry and fish when you finally have to eat fish. In general, the meat just needs to fill less on the plate than it does in many Danes today. Drink more red wine. Of course, you do not have to drink one glass after another, but you can replace the milk at dinner with a single glass of red wine. If you are missing out on inspiration, buy one of the many cookbooks that contain countless recipes for delicious Mediterranean dishes. Besides old age, factors about cardiovascular disease are the most frequent cause of death at home, Danes die every year from cardiovascular disease. Cardiovascular disease covers disorders of the heart, such as blood clots or heart cramps, as well as diseases of the body's arteries, including vein narrowing and atherosclerosis. Causes of cardiovascular disease are tobacco smoking, high cholesterol, narrowing the veins in the family, diabetes, high blood pressure, obesity, stress, and too little exercise.

There are several explanations of why the southern diet works. - The Mediterranean diet initiates a number of processes. It has a major impact on the cell layer that sits on the inside of the blood vessels. It is the cell layer that regulates how the vessels behave when a blood clot is formed. Much suggests that a Mediterranean diet goes in and helps that cellular layer prevent the occurrence of cardiovascular diseases such as blood clots, he says. If you know, eating a Mediterranean diet can get 30 percent. Reduction within the rate of heart attacks, this treatment is in line with what is seen in the best medical treatments. In the Spanish study, the test subjects were divided into three test groups. Two of the test groups were set to eat Mediterranean foods, where the diet was supplemented with extra virgin olive oil or nuts. The third group ate a low-fat diet. After five years, the number of blood clots, bleeding in the brain, as well as death caused by heart problems had decreased by 30 percent in the two test groups, where the subjects consumed Mediterranean food compared to the last test group. If you transfer the figures to Denmark, where you die from cardiovascular disease every year, thousands of lives can be saved by a simple dietary change. It makes an impression on Kenneth Egstrup: Great effect - If you eat a Mediterranean diet, you can get a 30 percent. Reduction in the number of heart attacks, this treatment is in line with what is seen in the best medical treatments, Kenneth Egstrup says, emphasizing that only the study was published in the highly acclaimed journal New England Journal of Medicine, how promising a result the Spanish scientists have achieved. Ulla Gregersen, the clinical dietitian, is also enthusiastic about the new research at the Heart Association: - The results are compelling because they measure not only cholesterol or blood pressure but death due to heart or bloodstream diseases.

The study shows how important the diet is in the prevention of cardiovascular disease.

Eat on holiday. Cut down on the red streaks and choose Mediterranean food, olive oil, nuts, and fish, instead. By Jeppe Helkov When thousands of Danes pack their bags for the summer and go to the south sun, a golden brown color should not be the only thing they bring home. The southern olive oil, the lean fish, and the fresh vegetables should also follow when moving home to another Danish rainy summer. A new Spanish study shows that Mediterranean Diet 4 should, in the future, be a permanent component of the Danish dinner table. The research project does investigate the impact of the Mediterranean diet on test subjects who had diabetes, high blood pressure, were overweight or had other similar deficiencies that brought them into the high-risk group for cardiovascular disease. The results show that thousands of Danish lives can be saved every year if you simply switch your diet to Mediterranean food. The red steaks must, therefore, be replaced with fish or poultry. The beers with a single glass of wine for the food. Dairy products with olive oil and nuts. And then you have to make sure to eat plenty of seasonal fruits and vegetables every day. Avoid blood clots. According to Kenneth Egstrup, chief physician at Svendborg Hospital, a specialist in heart disease.

Diversity Of Local Dishes

The "Cretan diet" or "Mediterranean diet" studied in public health for its health benefits designate the precise recommendations above and should not be confused with the diversity of diets of the different populations of the Mediterranean. There is no typical Mediterranean diet, there are more than twenty countries bordering the Mediterranean Sea, and dietary practices vary between countries and regions within countries. The health effects of each have not been systematically studied.

Even if this does not strictly concern the subject of this article on the Mediterranean diet, we can cite here the cuisines considered to be "Mediterranean":

• North of the Mediterranean Sea: the Provencal cuisine, the Languedoc cuisine, the Catalan cuisine, the Balkan cuisine - ex. : Albanian cuisine, Croatian cuisine, etc. - the Italian, Greek cuisine, and Turkish cuisine ;

- To the east Levantine cuisine (Syrian, Lebanese, Israeli, Cypriot and Palestinian);

- South the kitchen of the Maghreb countries: the Moroccan cuisine, the Tunisian cuisine, the Maltese cuisine, the Algerian cuisine, the Egyptian cuisine, the Libyan cuisine, or as the cooking Blackfoot ;

- West: the Spanish cuisine, the Portuguese cuisine.

Despite their differences, the Mediterranean countries have a partly common culinary culture: composition in food, but also culinary practices (importance of stuffing, puff pastry), common tastes for certain flavors (aromas of aromatic herbs, spices, taste for the tangy, sweet and sour...), but also a common idea of dietetics shared by Greek or Roman doctors of Antiquity (Hippocrates, Galen...), Persian doctors (Rhazès, Avicenne...), European doctors (Arnaud de Villeneuve, Aldebrandin de Sienne...).

History

This section is empty, insufficiently detailed, or incomplete. Your help is welcome! How to do it?

In 1948, the Rockefeller Foundation wanted to draw up an inventory of the health and living conditions of Crete's inhabitants after the Second World War. She found that their traditional diet, based on cereals, fruits, and vegetables, olives allowed Cretans to be healthy, despite the low consumption of animal products.

As early as the 1950s, interest in this diet was the subject of studies conducted among Cilento residents - by the American doctor Ancel Keys: his work established a major link between diet and cardiovascular disease. Ancel Keys describes the Mediterranean meal as "shared delights." Inseparable from his research, eating together is a fundamental component of the Mediterranean "lifestyle." It is an inherited secular quality:

"We don't sit at the table to eat but to eat together."

- said Plutarch in Ist century.

Today, this quality remains unchanged in several regions with a strong identity.

Cultural aspects

The "Mediterranean diet" was inscribed on November 16, 2010, on the representative list of the intangible cultural heritage of humanity by UNESCO as a "set of skills, knowledge, practices, and traditions." The inscription concerns four three communities linked by the same common cultural heritage and which are: Cilento (Italy), Coron (Greece), Soria (Spain), and Chefchaouen (Morocco). In 2013, three new countries were added by UNESCO: Cyprus, Croatia, and Portugal. These three countries are represented respectively by Agros' emblematic communities, the islands of Hvar and Brač, and the municipality of Tavira.

Health benefits

In general, the Mediterranean diet would allow greater longevity and a longer life expectancy in good health.

Evaluation difficulties

Its effectiveness is difficult to assess since it is essentially based on observational studies: unlike experimental studies, this is a case report where the cause and effect link cannot be established in the absence of external intervention. However, this study scheme is more suitable for the observation of rare diseases or for a long period between exposure and outcome.

Only a few studies are of an experimental type (the investigator voluntarily changes the eating habits of a group of patients). There are observations, in particular, of groups on the Greek island of Ikaria and in Sardinia.

Another technique is to compare the future in the same population of a group seriously following the diet and a group having abandoned.

Cardiovascular diseases

In 1970, a comparative study covering seven countries, chosen by the investigator, concluded that Cretan men had an exceptionally low rate of death from cardiovascular disease, despite a moderate to high consumption of fat.

Nearly 30 years later, a study called Lyon Diet Heart Study 8 tested a kind of Cretan diet pragmatically adapted to other cultures and lifestyle, after having found that a large part of the people followed by this study, only of patients who survived a first heart attack, would be reluctant to replace the butter with olive oil. Patients used rapeseed oil margarine and increased their intake of vitamin C- rich fruits by 20%and bread while reducing red and processed meats (cold cuts). This diet has led to a spectacular drop (-70%) in mortality from all causes. The success was such that the Ethics

Committee decided to discontinue the study prematurely to immediately make these results available to the public.

In terms of weight loss, it seems equivalent to other types of diet (low in fat or low in sugar) and provides better control of blood sugar.

In mid-2009, a study carried out in Greece concluded that two components of the Mediterranean diet (high consumption of vegetables and low consumption of meat) were more significantly associated with a lower risk of mortality than the other components of the diet (a diet rich in cereals and fish). In addition, moderate consumption of wine, high consumption of fruits and nuts, as well as pulses were also associated with a lower risk of mortality.

This diet could help keep a healthy brain by reducing mini-strokes' frequency that can contribute to mental decline.

The most positive effect seems to be a reduction in overall mortality, especially cardiovascular and cancer mortality (observational study). It seems to reduce the risk of the occurrence of cardiovascular diseases (interventional study). This reduction in cardiovascular diseases may be due to the improvement in risk factors as well as the risk of developing metabolic syndrome: obesity (interventional study), high blood pressure (observational study).

Neurological disorders

The Mediterranean diet does reduce the risk of developing Alzheimer's and Parkinson's disease by about one-fifth. In addition, this diet would reduce the risk of developing Alzheimer's disease (A.D.) but would also slow down its development, with a dose-response effect.

A sub-study of the PREDIMED trial shows that patients who randomly chose to receive a Mediterranean diet enriched with extra virgin olive oil or nuts have a better cognitive function than controls, which follow a diet low in fat.

The age-related cognitive decline in Spaniards at high cardiovascular risk was measured after six years of diet, either rich in olive oil and mixed nuts or a diet restricting fatty foods. The patients assigned to the nut plus olive oil diet not only had better cognitive scores than patients on the low-fat diet, but they had improved since the start of the study.

Others

Stricter adherence to the diet would be associated with a longer length of telomeres, which could promote longevity.

This diet, followed during pregnancy, seems to protect future children from asthma and allergies.

In addition, it would also finally facilitate the success of assisted fertilization; out of 161 women in couples treated for hypo fertility or infertility, pregnancies were in fact 40% more numerous in women who had followed a Mediterranean diet the best in the months preceding treatment (in vitro fertilization for 1/3 of them, and intracytoplasmic sperm injection for others). Women who followed a simple "healthy diet" (rich in fruits, vegetables, cereals, starchy foods, fish, low in meat, snack food, and mayonnaise, but less rich in olive oil than in the Mediterranean diet) a slightly worse result. The omega-6 fatty acids of olives are precursors of prostaglandins, which influence the menstrual cycle, ovulation, and the term to term of a pregnancy. The vitamin B6 was already known to improve the chances of fertilization among subfertile women. This type of study requires more scientific confirmation because biases here not controlled by scientists may exist, specify the authors.

Overall, the Mediterranean diet makes it possible to increase physical fitness, as can be seen from a faster walking speed.

It is important to distinguish this eating practice from "dieting" or "dieting" in common parlance, most of which prove to be counterproductive. At the end of these restrictive diets, the pounds lost are quickly regained, with overweight. Here it is more a way of life, sustainable, and whose benefits are felt in the short and medium-term.

Some characteristics of this diet are found in certain regions of the south of France and could, according to some authors, help to explain the French paradox.

These results mean that they inspire many official nutritional recommendations around the world.

Finally, the Mediterranean diet responds to the first recommendation of the "National Health Nutrition Program" (PNNS) of the INPES (National Institute for Prevention and Health Education): Eat fruits and vegetables per day. However, the PNNS is very different from the Mediterranean diet with regard to the recommendations for the consumption of meat and dairy products.

High protein diet

The high protein diet is based on the absorption of proteins by the body, limiting sugars and fats' intake through food. It is mainly intended for people who need to lose weight quickly for surgery or for health reasons. Weight loss is usually dramatic (up to 12 pounds per month). It is a low-calorie protein savings diet.

Principle

This slimming diet consists of drastically reducing the caloric intake in the form of carbohydrates and lipids while preventing muscle wasting by suitable protein intake. It consists of a diet naturally rich in protein made from lean meat, egg white, fish, and dairy products. It is also possible to obtain a high-protein diet based on plant-based foods (nuts, beans, quinoa, soy, and tofu, among others). However, as these foods are less rich in amino acids and the proteins they contain are less easily absorbable, a higher protein intake (up to + 25%) is recommended 2. Protein can also be obtained from powdered preparations in the form of high-protein sachets. It is thus necessary to ingest from 50 to 100 grams of proteins per day. Protein requirements are around 1g per day and per kilogram of bodyweight to preserve muscle mass.

Note: proteins do not make you lose weight: it is the decrease in the intake of lipids and carbohydrates that will allow weight loss; proteins will only help ensure the vital functions of the body.

Plan limit

Many criticisms are made regarding this diet. The first is that proteins are themselves energy sources for the human body through the Krebs cycle. The human body metabolizes them and can transform them into fats and carbohydrates. In fact, the overabsorption of protein beyond the amount needed by the body (between 1 and 2% of the amount of protein in the body per day) generates energy production. In the case of overabundance, the diet can, therefore, lead to additional fat storage.

Among the disadvantages, we can note deficiencies and various risks without medical monitoring. The deficiencies must be prevented by suitable food supplements and, in particular, vitamins, potassium, magnesium, calcium, and sodium. The diet being very low in lipids, we generally recommend the addition of Omega 3, which is an essential fatty acid that is likely to be quickly lacking in the body. The high protein diet may be contraindicated in some cases. Do not hesitate to consult your doctor before undertaking it.

The extreme absorption of proteins (more than 200 g per day), coupled with the inadequate absorption of other sources of calories (fat or carbohydrates), can cause a form of metabolic disturbance that can go as far as death, known as the name of caribou evil. Even when combined with other sources of calories, consuming more than 285 g of protein per day (for an 80 kg person) can be dangerous.

Health Is The State Of Mind And Body

It is important to take care of both your mind and your body. It will benefit you in various ways, including:

☐   Allow you to take absolute control of your life and feel good about the choices you make.

☐   Gain energy and feel fit.

☐   Improve your physical health.

☐   Win a positive outlook and enjoy your life more.

Any change in lifestyle is a "work in progress." Lasting changes take time. Therefore, start by setting small goals that are easy to incorporate into your daily life and can control. Well-being and physical fitness involve being aware and making healthy decisions about diet and exercise and staying positive.

Here Are The Main Nutritional Rules Of The Mediterranean Diet

• Plants at will

Fruit and vegetables at all meals, in good quantity, raw or cooked, dried fruits and oilseeds are also welcome! Vary the colors and always choose seasonal plants.

• Starchy foods and pulses

These are the primary sources of energy for this diet. Preferably full, starchy foods are included in most meals. Cereals and pulses are preferred, not to mention the tubers.

• Olive oil as the best ally

Olive oil can be consumed in all sauces, when cooked, alone, or served (for example, rapeseed oil). It replaces butter and other fats.

• Quality animal proteins

Large or small fish, seafood, or even seaweed seafood are eaten regularly, as are eggs from hens raised outdoors or flax seeds. White meat is also on the menu but without abuse. Red meat, cold meats occupy a less important place. You can, however, follow a vegetarian Mediterranean diet.

• Dairy products in moderate quantities

The Mediterranean regions are not breeding grounds, but there are still flocks of sheep or goats there. This is why dairy products are part of the Mediterranean diet, in moderate quantities, and rather in the form of fresh cheeses and yogurt. Favor dairy products from goats or sheep.

• A little alcohol during meals

One glass of red wine at each meal is allowed.

What food, how often?

Once these broad lines have been set out, what to do in practice? Here are consumption benchmarks for each food family.

A Recent Study Carried Out On Primates Highlights The Effects On Hunger, Weight, Metabolism And Hepatic Fat Of A Mediterranean Diet Compared To A Classic Western Diet.

Why it matters

The Mediterranean diet is generally considered one of the best for health. We know this through various observational studies, several clinical trials, and other experiments on specific compounds contained in the foods that make up this diet. However, studies on humans are often complicated to carry out (the problem of patient monitoring, the accuracy of food intake, etc.)

Therefore, researchers undertook an experiment on primates (whose genes are very close to ours) for more than two years. Details.

The study

For 38 weeks, scientists studied the impact of a diet mimicking the composition of a Mediterranean diet or a typical Western diet on calorie consumption, fat mass, energy expended, physical activity, insulin resistance, and hepatic fats carbohydrate metabolism, and triglyceride levels of 43 primates.

Results: the Western diet increased caloric intake during the first six months, as well as body fat, activity, energy expenditure, insulin resistance, and fatty liver after two and a half years of follow-up, while the Mediterranean diet did not have these effects but reduced triglyceride levels.

An editorial on the study indicates a potential factor that could be responsible for stopping the increase in energy consumption beyond the first six months: the RGS4 gene, a gene regulating food intake. This gene is abnormal in obesity. Therefore, it would be interesting to know if the monkeys who ate more throughout the experiment had an abnormality of this gene compared to those who regulated their intakes after six months.

Finally, this is the first study in controlled experimental conditions showing a difference in caloric intake and weight and fat gain associated with a Western diet's long-term adoption against a Mediterranean diet. It is also the first experimental evidence that a Mediterranean diet could protect against fatty liver disease (compared to the typical Western diet).

In practice

Now there is sufficient evidence to promote the Mediterranean diet as a whole. However, it should not be forgotten that she is inseparable from her lifestyle and that the other activities associated with it (physical activity, stress management, social ties, etc.) are also beneficial for health.

Adopting this diet may notably reduce the risk of cardiovascular and metabolic diseases provided that it consists of raw and minimally processed products.

Five Reasons To Adopt The Mediterranean Diet

Balanced, easy to follow, the Mediterranean diet has it all: good for the line; it keeps your body and mind healthy and makes you live longer.

Vegetables, fruits, cereals, legumes, fish, olive oil, nuts, spices, and a little red wine are the Mediterranean diet bases. However, this diet limits the consumption of red meat, processed foods, and sugar. Here are five good reasons to join.

To live longer in good health.

We attribute to the Mediterranean diet many virtues, including that of making us live longer: it would indeed reduce all-cause mortality by 37%. It is associated with a decrease in mortality from cancer by 36% and mortality from cardiovascular disease by 32%. In the same way, compared to those who follow a "typical" Western diet, women who follow a Mediterranean diet are 40% more likely to be over 70 years old while being in better health.

To protect his heart.

In particular, it is reducing the cardiovascular risk that the Mediterranean diet makes it possible to extend life expectancy. At the beginning of the 1990s, the Lyon Diet Heart Study, conducted by Michel de Lorgeril and Serge Renaud, proved the interest for patients at cardiovascular risk of adopting a Mediterranean diet rich in omega-3 (acid alpha-linolenic).

Since then, numerous studies have confirmed these discoveries. For example, this is shown by a study carried out on 7447 people aged 55 to 80 at a supposedly high cardiovascular risk but with no history. The researchers looked firstly at the Mediterranean diet's effects on myocardial infarction, stroke, cardiovascular mortality. Compared to a the low-fat diet, the Mediterranean diet enriches nuts or olive oil, significantly reducing the incidence of major cardiovascular events. The benefit is particularly clear when it comes to stroke.

The Mediterranean diet is beneficial thanks to its richness in fruits and vegetables in olive oil, while its low glycemic index, low sugar content, and its richness in fibers and polyphenols contribute to decreasing inflammation and glycemia, risk factors in cardiovascular diseases.

To stay in shape

A new study of 16,000 people followed for ten years shows that the Mediterranean diet can reduce the risk of obesity by 43%. These results were presented to the European Congress on Obesity in Porto. By analyzing the diet of the participants, the researchers found that the higher the proportion of fruits, vegetables, and legumes, the lower the risk of becoming obese, compared to those who consumed more meat and animal fats. Those who had the lowest risk of obesity did not completely exclude meat but had much lower intakes than people who had a conventional diet. They also ate a lot of fish.

To preserve your brain.

The Mediterranean diet would protect the brain from aging and limit age-related cognitive decline. It promotes cognitive skills in seniors by delaying, in particular, the shrinking of the brain during aging. In recent years, various studies have identified a link between the Mediterranean diet and a reduced risk of age-related diseases such as dementia. Twelve of them were analyzed by a team of researchers. In 9 out of 12 studies, the Mediterranean diet was associated with better cognitive function, less cognitive decline, and a reduced risk of Alzheimer's disease. However, there were no significant findings regarding mild cognitive impairment.

The Mediterranean diet benefits come in part from fish omega-3 fatty acids that keep nerve cells healthy, red wine, and other sources of antioxidants and group B vitamins that can help slow down atrophy of the brain. In the same way, limiting meat, especially grilled meat, makes it possible to reduce glycation products' consumption, implicated in the risk of dementia.

To decrease the risk of cancer.

Followers of the Mediterranean diet have a 33% lower risk of stomach cancer. This is what a study of around 500,000 people in 10 countries reports. Another study carried out on 62,573 participants showed that postmenopausal women who follow a Mediterranean type diet have a markedly reduced risk of an aggressive form of breast cancer, those who do not express estrogen receptors.

One explanation for the Mediterranean diet's protective role is its high content of antioxidants (vitamins C and E, phenolic compounds, terpenes), which reduces oxidative stress and the risk of chronic diseases associated with it.

Vegetarian Diet Balance

Plant Protein Quality

A balanced vegetarian diet involves eating a wide range of foods in the proper amount. There is a certain list of nutrients that you should pay special attention to if you intend to refuse animal origin food. The most important of these is protein. Lacto-ovarian and ovarian vegetarians receive high-quality protein with food, and protein deficiency in their body is unlikely.

At the same time, people who use only products of plant origin can experience a protein deficiency if they do not maintain a balance of essential (essential) amino acids in their diet. The fact is that the structure of plant proteins lacks one or more essential amino acids.

It was previously believed that the entire complex of essential amino acids should be present in every meal. However, the modern approach allows for a large variance in the intake of amino acids included in this complex - we are talking more about days than hours. Thus, the vegetarian diet should be balanced for essential amino acids, and the time between their meals can be a day or more.

Researchers have discovered that if the food intake is poor in essential amino acids, the liver can break down its own protein to make up for their shortage. Moreover, as soon as a sufficient amount of essential amino acids reappears in the diet, the liver restores its own protein reserves.

Since each individual type of plant food does not contain a full complex of essential amino acids, it is important for a vegetarian to plan his diet so that some proteins complement others. For example, in most cereals, the level of the essential amino acid lysine is very low, while in legumes, the level of sulfur-containing amino acids is quite low.

Thus, by combining these two groups of products (for example, using canned beans and corn tortillas), a vegetarian can provide the entire complex of amino acids to his body and achieve in this regard an effect similar to eating high-quality animal protein.

Vitamin B12

Another nutrient that could be deficient in a vegetarian diet is vitamin B12. Especially, this fact applies to athletes who adhere to a strictly vegetarian diet (vegans). Rauma and colleagues (1995) studied the presence of vitamin B12 in the body of those people who practiced raw foods (eating only plant foods in raw form). Most foods in this diet are fermented or sprouted (grains). In this case, the concentration of vitamin B12 in the blood plasma of the 21st participant of the experiment was similar to the concentration of this vitamin in the blood of the 21st participant of the control group, who ate meat.

However, a long-term study showed a decrease in plasma vitamin B12 levels in 6 out of 9 participants.

The cross-sectional analysis revealed a significantly lower content of B12 in the blood of vegans than in the blood of the control group.

Those study participants who consumed nori algae had generally higher vitamin B12 content than other vegans. But in the long run, all but one of these participants finally got a lower B12. Despite the fact that, in general, fewer vitamins B12 were found in the body of vegans, only in a few cases could we talk about the clinical deficiency of this nutrient.

Helman and Darnthill (1987) conducted a study in which the average vitamin B12 level in plasma of vegetarians was 350 pg/ml, in people on a mixed diet - 490 pg/ml, and only 16% of vegetarians had a level of B12 below 200 pg/ml.

B12 deficiency is rarely observed in lacto-overo-vegetarians since milk and eggs contain a sufficient amount of this nutrient. Vegans can also recommend the use of soy milk enriched with B12 vitamins. Analogs of this vitamin, in their natural form, contained in seaweed, spirulina, nori, as well as fermented soy products, do not have the proper effect on the human body.

Patients with a clinical deficiency of vitamin B12 may show signs of paresthesia (numbness and tingling in the extremities), feel weak, dizzy, lose their orientation in space, and they may also develop psychiatric disorders, such as depression or memory loss. In addition, the use of alcohol, tobacco, as well as antacids, neomycin, colchicine, aminosalicylic acid can cause problems with the absorption of vitamin B12 in the body of both vegetarians and ordinary people.

The presence of iron in a vegetarian diet

In general, both vegetarians and ordinary athletes may experience an iron deficiency in the body. At the same time, those who eat red meat are less exposed to this risk. In absolute terms, red meat contains a fairly average amount of iron, while the bioavailability of iron from red meat is higher than from plant sources. In general, the iron contained in the products can be divided into two types: organic (heme) and inorganic (non-heme).

Hem iron contained in meat, fish, and poultry is better absorbed than non-heme iron found in cereals, vegetables, fruits.

Absorption of heme and non-heme iron in the human body varies from 3% to 35%, depending on factors such as the presence of ascorbic acid in the human body, the source of iron (heme or heme), as well as its own iron stores in the body.

Iron is classified as an essential nutrient and is involved in the formation of hemoglobin and myoglobin, as well as hemoproteins, which are found in all cells of the body and catalyze redox reactions. Iron is also a co-factor in a number of enzymatic reactions, including reactions involved in the synthesis of collagen and various neurotransmitters. In addition, iron is an essential factor for the normal functioning of the immune system and is involved in the detoxification of the body.

Since iron plays an important role in redox processes, it is extremely important for an athlete to maintain the necessary level of this element in the body.

There are two different approaches to determining an iron deficiency in athletes. The first is to measure the level of ferritin in the blood plasma; the second is to measure the level of hemoglobin and hematocrit.

The percentage of athletes suffering from iron deficiency is difficult to calculate.

In the 80s and early 90s, the debate was caused by the fact that athletes who ate little heme iron and had small iron stores in the body, nevertheless, did not show any decrease in performance. However, researchers recommend continuous monitoring of iron in the body of athletes, especially female athletes. In particular, the sports department of the U.S. Olympic Committee recommends a hemoglobin and hematocrit screening twice a year.

Snyder and colleagues (1989) investigated the effects of mixed and vegetarian diets on iron in women athletes. The study groups were selected according to the criteria of age, body weight, aerobic performance, the number of training loads, and the number of previous pregnancies.

The so-called group of "modified vegetarians" (of 9 people) actually consumed meat, but in the amount of not more than 100 g per week, while the control group (also of 9 people) included red meat in their diet on an ongoing basis.

Both groups received the same amount of iron with food (14 mg per day), but the plasma ferritin level and the body's ability to bind iron were significantly lower in "modified vegetarians" (P <0.05). In addition, the authors found that the bioavailability of iron in the diet of the first and second groups was different.

Iron, which was consumed by "modified vegetarians," was much less readily available for absorption by the body than iron, which ingested by the control group. This suggests that in the body of women runners, heme iron is absorbed much well than non-heme iron.

The results of these case studies have also been confirmed for non-athletes. So, in 1995, Shaw and colleagues examined 55 Chinese Buddhist vegetarians (23 men and 32 women) for iron in the body. Non-vegetarian students (20 men and 39 women) acted as a control group. Among the parameters that were to be measured were the amount of iron contained in the participants' diet, as well as the content of hemoglobin, iron in the blood plasma, the level of transferrin saturation with iron, and the level of ferritin in the blood plasma. In addition, a general biochemical blood test was performed.

Most of the protein in the Buddhist vegetarian diet was ingested with soybeans, which contain a fairly small amount of bioavailable iron. Daily intake of iron was similar among male vegetarians and non-vegetarians, while female vegetarians consumed significantly more iron than non-vegetarians. The analysis showed that the median concentration of ferritin in the blood plasma of vegetarians is only half of the same indicator in the blood of non-vegetarians. In addition, in the group of vegetarians, there were more participants with a lower plasma ferritin level, especially for female vegetarians.

Nutrition Strategies to Increase Iron in Vegetarian Nutrition

So, food of animal origin is the source of the most accessible for the absorption of iron. This is a problem for vegetarians who do not eat meat products and, in particular red meat.

Lacto-ovarian vegetarians also have trouble getting enough iron into their bodies since dairy products are fairly poor in iron. In this case, it is recommended that more green vegetables, such as spinach or some legumes, as well as whole-grain cereals specially enriched with iron, be included in the diet. A substantial amount of iron is found in dried fruits. In addition, it is recommended to cook in iron dishes. When acidic foods are cooked in iron dishes, part of the iron goes into the food.

Zinc in the body of vegetarian athletes

The best sources of zinc in the diet are meat and dairy, and seafood (especially oysters). That is why vegetarians need to pay special attention to the intake of this element in the body. Whole-grain cereals are one of the main sources of zinc in vegetarian diets, but the high fiber content in cereals reduces the bioavailability of zinc.

Zinc is found in almost all body tissues and is a co-factor for more than 100 enzymes, some of which play an important role in the process of energy synthesis. Zinc is also required for protein synthesis and is an integral part of the insulin molecule.

Some studies have shown that exercise leads to increased loss of zinc by the human body. This suggests that the level of zinc in the body of athletes may be lower than in ordinary people.

The lack of zinc within the body can be caused by various factors, including insufficient intake of zinc from food, its low bioavailability, increased loss of zinc by the body during exercise, a general increase in blood plasma volume, redistribution of zinc among body tissues.

However, Lukaski, in his work, refuted the results of these studies and showed that the level of zinc in the human body does not decrease during training if, at the same time, its intake in the body is at an adequate level. Lukaski and colleagues studied 16 women and 13 male swimmers. The control group included 13 women and 15 male non-swimmers.

At the same time, the level of zinc in the blood plasma remained at a constant normal level throughout the training season. In addition to studies, Lucaschi, Duster, and colleagues investigated the effect of zinc on the endurance of 13 trained women athletes. The control group consisted of 10 untrained women. At the same time, an analysis of food intake was carried out over a 3-day period for the presence of zinc; in addition, blood and urine tests were performed 24 hours before and after taking 25 mg of zinc orally.

The average daily intake of zinc with food did not differ much and was generally lower than the recommended daily intake in both the main and control groups. The authors did not notice any significant differences in fasting analyzes of the level of zinc, serum albumin, a-2-macroglobulin in blood plasma, as well as zinc bound by red blood cells. However, in trained female athletes, it was noted ($P < 0.05$) that a greater amount of zinc was excreted in the urine, and in addition, a less pronounced response to oral intake of zinc was recorded. The authors suggested that a larger amount of zinc excreted in the urine may be due to accelerated muscle metabolism.

Zinc and Vegetarians

Several other authors have also noted a deficiency of zinc in vegetarians. Janelle and Barr report on a study among women vegetarians (vegans and lacto-vegetarians) regarding the presence of zinc in the body.

The control group consisted of women on a mixed diet. It was found that the level of zinc consumed by vegans and lacto-vegetarians is lower (8.5 mg and 8.2 mg per day, respectively) than the recommended daily allowance (15 mg per day).

Similar results were viewed by studies conducted by Donovan and Gibson (1995), which found that 33% of semi-vegetarians, 24% of Lacto-overo-vegetarians, and 18% of omnivores, plasma levels of zinc were lower than 10.7 nMol/liter. It was found that the ratio of the level of phytates to the level of zinc in food consumed negatively correlates with the concentration of zinc in blood plasma (P <0.05). The authors concluded that the low level of zinc in the body of the studied is primarily due to its low content in the consumed food and its poor bioavailability. Moreover, this is true for all studied groups.

Eating Zinc Strategies

The largest amount of zinc contains products such as oysters, crab, shrimp, legumes, wheat germ. In addition, you can pay attention to products such as nuts, legumes, whole grain products. At the same time, refined flour is poor in zinc.

Calcium is a Vegetarian Diet

The diet of a typical vegetarian contains a small amount of calcium, with the exception of dairy products and dark greens. As in the case of iron and zinc, calcium absorption can be hampered by the presence of phytates, oxalates, fiber, and tannins in food. Phytic acid is found in oatmeal and other whole grain cereals, oxalates are present in large quantities in spinach, beets, and greens. These elements bind calcium and make it difficult to absorb. Therefore, those athletes who adhere to a strictly vegetarian diet and receive calcium mainly from whole grain cereals and greens are at risk, unlike lacto-vegetarians, to face a calcium deficiency in the body.

In addition, with a strictly vegetarian diet, vitamin D deficiency usually manifests itself, which also negatively affects the absorption and utilization of calcium.

In 1992, Gonzalez-Reimers and Arnalay de la Rosa conducted an interesting anthropological study of pre-Hispanic burials in the Canary Islands. Among the 117 skeletons excavated by scientists, a significant amount was discovered with signs of osteoporosis. Analysis of bones for the presence of traces of various elements showed a low concentration of zinc, iron, and copper in them. It was noted that trabecular bone mass was presented below normal.

The authors report that in pre-Hispanic times, the Canary Islands dwelled mainly on protein-poor foods and herbal products made up the bulk of the diet. This, according to the researchers, could ultimately lead to the development of osteoporosis.

In this regard, the authors recommend that vegetarians who do not consume dairy products pay attention to foods containing calcium supplements, such as, for example, calcium-fortified soy products. In addition, they recommend consuming more dark greens.

Another Mediterranean Diet Weekly Menu

The Mediterranean Diet is more than a diet; it is a whole philosophy of life-based on a different way of feeding ourselves, cooking food, sharing them, and enjoying our surroundings. A diet in which what we eat is as important as the way we do it.

Declared by the UNESCO Intangible Cultural Heritage of Humanity, however, in few countries, the adherence to the Mediterranean Diet has decreased significantly, being the second country, after Greece that has moved further away from it. At present, the contribution of fat has increased and, when four decades ago it constituted only 25% of the diet, it now accounts for 40%.

However, when Spaniards are asked if they follow a Mediterranean Diet, 41% of respondents respond that they follow it often, 21% follow it, and 26% think that it follows it sometimes or never.

Therefore it is important to recover our own eating habits, buy fresh and seasonal products and prepare them ourselves in a simple way, as are most of the dishes of the extensive Mediterranean recipe — a style of food like this weekly menu proposed by the Mediterranean Diet Foundation.

MONDAY

• Breakfast: Coffee with milk. Toast with goat cheese spread. Apple.

• Mid-morning: cereal bar. Natural Orange Juice

• Food: Chickpea soup. Hake meatballs stewed with potatoes. Grapes.

• Snack: Cottage cheese with sugar.

• Dinner: Swiss chard with garlic. Grilled turkey and tomato cherry skewers with couscous. Custard apple.

TUESDAY

- Breakfast: Milk with cocoa powder. Whole grains

- Mid-morning: Natural pear smoothie.

- Food: Stewed green beans. Grilled chicken fillet with steamed broccoli. Pineapple Carpaccio.

- Snack: Toast with quince jam.

- Dinner: Salad with cucumber, black olives, onion, and Feta cheese. Salmon with papillote vegetables. Peach.

WEDNESDAY

- Breakfast: Milk Crispbread with strawberry jam.

- Mid-morning: Sandwich with lettuce, tomato, and cheese. Natural grape juice.

- Food: Tomato soup. Broth rice with rabbit and artichokes. Orange.

- Snack: Seed bread with olive oil.

• Dinner: Cauliflower sauteed with bacon. Scrambled eggs with roasted mushrooms. Banana with yogurt.

THURSDAY

• Breakfast: Milk Olive bread with slices of tomato and virgin olive oil.

• Mid-morning: Apple compote.

• Food: Roasted red peppers with pine nuts. Grilled pork loin with mustard and rice sauce. Khaki.

• Snack: Tuna mini sandwich.

• Dinner: Vegetable cream with croutons. Fried fish. Tangerines

FRIDAY

• Breakfast: Coffee with milk. Toast with chocolate spread.

• Mid-morning: Muesli with dried fruit.

• Food: Stewed beans. Tortilla with vegetables and peas (Campesina) with lettuce. Grapes.

- Snack: Milk. Homemade cake.

- Dinner: Sauteed Brussels sprouts with chopped almonds. Spinach, goat cheese, and honey crepe with zucchini slices. Pear.

SATURDAY

- Breakfast: Integral cookies. Pineapple yogurt smoothie.

- Mid-morning: Appetizer: assorted montaditos.

- Food: Migas. Nice pickled with onion. Banana flambé with chocolate.

- Snack: Macedonia.

- Dinner: Two-color puree (potato and beet) gratin. Baked carrot chicken thighs. Orange.

SUNDAY

- Breakfast: Coffee with milk. Ensaimada

- Mid-morning: Appetizer: assorted nuts, dried fruits, and olives.

- Food: Vegetable cannelloni au gratin. Grilled duck breast with fig sauce. Orange with custard

- Snack: Apple rolled with cinnamon.

- Dinner: Fine noodle soup. Eggs stuffed with smoked salmon gratin with grated carrot. Fruit frozen yogurt.

It is also important to enjoy the family meal and exercise. In short, be Mediterranean again.

Food outside the Mediterranean Diet.

Sausages, butter, and sweets should only be consumed occasionally or even excluded in the context of a Mediterranean diet. Fried food and processed products. Generally, they are not part of this diet.

Mediterranean Diet for The Heart

The Mediterranean diet minimizes the risk of cardiovascular disease. This is because olive oil, a key ingredient in this regimen, contains monounsaturated fatty acids that increase HDL rates. Good cholesterol

Mediterranean Diet against Breast Cancer

Diets protect women from breast cancer, according to a study. On average, the reduction in the incidence of the disease, which researchers found after the adoption of the Mediterranean diet, was 62%.

Conclusion

Several studies are positive about the Mediterranean diet. The diet would, for example, be conducive to people with diabetes, high cholesterol, or high blood pressure. This way of eating could even improve your memory and combat depression. It would be the combination of the different aspects of the diet that make it healthy. So this would be a better way to eat than to focus on specific 'superfoods' or to exclude certain categories, such as sugars, ultimately.

By adding an extra spoon of olive oil to an unhealthy meal, you will not suddenly become healthier. Combining olive oil with lots of vegetables, lean meat, and whole-grain pasta can do wonders for your health. The Mediterranean kitchen, therefore, ensures the right balance.

In January 2019, the Mediterranean diet was named "Best Diet for 2019" by U.S. News & World Report. The DASH diet came in second place, followed by 'flexitarian' food.

CPSIA information can be obtained
at www.ICGtesting.com
Printed in the USA
BVHW091939240421
605722BV00004B/1087

9 781801 271004